USING DESKTOP PUBLISHING TO CREATE NEWSLETTERS, HANDOUTS, AND WEB PAGES

A How-To-Do-It Manual

John Maxymuk

HOW-TO-DO-IT MANUALS
FOR LIBRARIANS

NUMBER 74

NEAL-SCHUMAN PUBLISHERS, INC.
New York, London

Images used in this book are protected by copyright by the following companies:
Computer Support Corporation, T/Maker Company, New Vision Technologies, and
Marketing Graphics Incorporated. The author gratefully acknowledges their agree-
ment to publishing their materials.

Published by Neal-Schuman Publishers, Inc.
100 Varick Street
New York, NY 10013

Printed and bound in the United States of America.

Library of Congress Cataloging-in-Publication Data

Maxymuk, John.
   Using desktop publishing to create newsletters, handouts, and Web
pages : a how-to-do-it manual for librarians / by John Maxymuk.
      p.   cm.—(How-to-do-it manuals for librarians ; no. 74)
   Includes bibliographical references (p.) and index.
   ISBN 1-55570-265-1
   1. Libraries—United States—Data processing. 2. Desktop publishing—
United States. 3. Libraries—United States—Handbooks, manuals, etc.—
Data processing. 4. Newsletters—United States—Data manuals for
libraries ; no. 74.
Z678.93.D46M39   1997
686.2'2544536'024092—dc21
                                                        97-3980

This book is for the three who believe in me most, the three whom I believe in devotedly: Suzanne, Juliane, and Katie

CONTENTS

FIGURES

Illustrations in the above figures were taken from the following sources

Arts & Letters Jurassic Art
© 1993 Computer Support Corporation
Figures 4.3, 4.4, 4.5, 4.6, 4.7

ClickArt
© 1993 T/Maker Company
Figures 4.1, 7.8, 11.13, 12.3, 12.5, 12.8

Presentation Task Force
© 1991 New Vision Technologies, Inc.
Figures 2.2, 4.2, 6.5, 7.3, 7.7

Publisher's Picture Pak
© 1987 Marketing Graphics Incorporated
Figures 2.1, 6.15, 7.2, 7.4, 7.7

Sandra's Clip Art Server
http://seidel.ncsa.uiuc.edu/ClipArt/
Figures 11.6, 11.7, 11.9, 11.11, 11.13

PREFACE

The need for libraries to communicate information is clear. What should be equally clear is the need to communicate effectively so that the message sent is the message received. This is where desktop publishing comes in. Desktop publishing puts the power and possibilities of publishing, of sharing information with the public, on an individual's desktop. It's easy; it's fun; but there are guidelines to follow to do so effectively. *Using Desktop Publishing to Create Newsletters, Handouts, and Web Pages* is about those guidelines.

This book is divided into four sections. The chapters in the first section provide an overview of the basic elements of desktop publishing. There, the reader can find information on the hardware and software necessary for both minimum and optimum operations. In this section, one can also learn the basic elements of design. Effective design is the primary difference between a publication that is used and one that is thrown away. The building blocks of design outlined here are layout, type fonts, and graphic elements such as illustrations and photographs.

Sections 2, 3, and 4 deal with specific library applications for desktop publishing: library guides, organizational newsletters, and World Wide Web home pages. While each incorporates the basic principles outlined in section 1, there are significant differences among these types of publications. Planning, producing, and publishing library guides pose different challenges from those of newsletters. A Web page, which exists primarily in the ether of cyberspace and is accessible essentially to the entire world, is a whole new species with entirely new properties and challenges entirely separate from the world of paper.

The examples in this book were created largely with PageMaker and WordPerfect in a Windows environment, because that is what I have on my desktop. There are many other fine programs available for both Mac and Windows environments, however, and this book is not intended to be a primer on either PageMaker or WordPerfect. As such, specific program commands generally are not addressed; instead, the focus is on a practical discussion of the issues of desktop publishing.

The overall aim of *Using Desktop Publishing to Create Newsletters, Handouts, and Web Pages: A How-To-Do-It Manual* is to help readers create their own publications and to make those publications look sharp, read well, and be used. Whether it's an instructional library guide for patrons, a newsletter for an institution or professional association, or a home page mounted on the World Wide Web, a smart, attractive publication speaks highly of the librarians who created it and the library it represents.

ACKNOWLEDGMENTS

Some special thanks are in order to those who helped get this project into print. Thanks to my colleagues at the Paul Robeson Library for providing me with the time to write this manuscript, and to Ken Kuehl, Olga Moore, Mike Moyers, and Julie Still for reading the draft and commenting on it. Thanks also to the Philadelphia Area Reference Librarians' Information Exchange (PARLIE), the Documents Association of New Jersey (DANJ), and Burlington County Bank for letting me refine my newsletter ideas through years of practice. Thanks to Temple University and Rutgers University library systems for allowing me to do the same for library guides and Web pages. Thanks to Charles Harmon and the rest of the fine folks at Neal-Schuman who have done such a nice job on both projects I have completed with them. Finally, a loving thanks to my mother and father for selflessly raising me, my wife for faithfully humoring me, and my daughters just for being with me.

INTRODUCTION: GETTING STARTED WITH DESKTOP PUBLISHING

Before the advent of desktop publishing in the 1980s, the process for printing and publishing was time-consuming, specialized, and involved the coordinated work of several people. An editor might assign writers to write copy, which then would be reviewed by copyeditors. The edited copy would be given to a typesetter to be electronically set into type. Typefaces and graphic elements were the responsibility of the designer, and the whole publication would then be laid out using laborious cut-and-paste methods, by the layout artist. Any errors then spotted by the proofreader could throw the whole production into turmoil and make it a late night for everyone as a deadline approached.

While a library publication might compress the editing and writing stages of the process, the edited copy still needed to go to a professional printer in order to look presentable. The only alternative was the typewriter-and-photocopier combination. Any special graphical elements would have to be added through an amateurish attempt at cut-and-paste.

Desktop publishing allows you to transfer some, most, or even all of the procedures described above to one personal computer on one desktop. How much of the process is transferred to your desktop depends on how much technology you can afford and master, how professional your publication needs to look, and how big your budget is. You may not have a laser or color printer and may instead deliver your publication to the printer as a file on a disk. Or you may take the camera-ready, laser-printed originals of the pages of your publication to a good quality photocopier because the publication is mostly black text on white paper with few fancy graphic elements. If you have some grayscale graphics that just won't show up well on a standard photocopy, then you may deliver camera-ready, laser-printed originals to your printer to be professionally printed because of the higher quality reproduction. Today, the choice is yours.

As these examples show, desktop publishing is employed to different degrees by different people. Its defining feature is that it puts the power of publishing on your desktop. How much of that power you use is up to you. Desktop publishing gives you as much control over the process and the look of the final publication as you want. It allows you to combine text, images, tables, charts, and much more from many different sources into one computer file and, ultimately, one attractive publication. It can save you time and money in producing materials. It can also be fun.

However, desktop publishing is not cheap; the startup costs for hardware and software can be considerable. It also requires real skill, or more precisely, a set of real skills. The person or team responsible for desktop publishing in your organization needs to be able to write well, edit even better, and work with copy, typefaces, and graphic elements with the eye of a designer. It takes time; the efforts of someone who is either dabbling or rushed will be painfully obvious. A great deal of thought must go into any publication, no matter how small.

BASIC CONSIDERATIONS

When embarking on any sort of publishing venture, a number of factors must be taken into account. That is true whether the projected publication be a newsletter, a library handout, a page on the World Wide Web (WWW), or the book you are currently reading. These considerations are really questions that can be divided into two categories: (1) general questions concerning the overall goals of the project, and (2) detailed questions concerning exactly how the project will be completed.

GENERAL QUESTIONS

What is the goal of this project? What message are you trying to convey? To whom are you trying to convey this message? How can this audience best be reached? These are the sorts of general questions that need to be addressed.

Answers to the first two questions should be obvious if you are serious about continuing with the project. The goal should be to communicate information to a target audience. That information could be instructions on using a reference tool, announcements of upcoming meetings, reports on topics of interest, or many other things that you or your organization want to share. The message might best be accomplished by long, thoughtful pieces of text, or by short items of interest. It might consist of brief, factual reference material, or information the reader is not interested in but needs to be aware of. If the message is not clearly expressed, then the best technology and design won't produce an effective publication.

The harder questions to answer are those pertaining to your

audience. Who are they? What are they like? What do they want to see? What do they want to know? What do they need to know? How can you best use the techniques of desktop publishing to reach them?

If you were in the business world, now would be the time for market research—expensive, detailed surveying of the target audience's demographic makeup, views, and preferences. This sort of research is not generally an option for libraries, although small local surveys are possible. It is more likely that you will rely on your firsthand knowledge of a sampling of the target audience. Whether your audience consists of students, faculty, community patrons, colleagues, or others, you know and have dealt with a fair number of these users all along and can describe what their interests, concerns, and knowledge levels are and what that means for your publication. Even if you are trying to reach nonlibrary users, you can put yourself in their shoes and imagine how best to attract and reach them as well. You would also do well to study other publications of a similar nature to see what works and what doesn't.

Once you have mentally responded to these general questions, you are ready to face detailed questions on the nitty gritty elements of production.

DETAILED QUESTIONS

The first consideration here is, who is going to do all of this? Who is going to write the text? Who will edit the text? Who will design the publication? Who will lay it out electronically? Who will proof the publication for errors?

In the library world, where budgets tend to be tight and areas of responsibility tend to be wide, the answer to all of the above questions is likely to be you and you alone. And it is equally likely that these new desktop publishing duties will be added to your existing responsibilities without a consequent reduction of the current workload. However, the bright side is that desktop publishing can be so much fun that it can give an exhilarating boost to the everyday particulars of your workday. And if you're good at it, you'll probably be asked to do more of it, raising both your profile and that of the library or organization for whom you're working. The flip side to that is that you may get so good at it that your desktop publishing skills are constantly in demand both at work and home. You may be making a lifetime commitment without realizing it.

Since you are the person in charge of this project, what you need to know next is how much money is budgeted for it. How much can you afford to do? Do you need to buy computer hardware or software? If it's going to be a paper publication, what kind of paper will you use? How many pages will it be? What weight of paper will you use? What paper size? Will you use white or colored paper? Will the publication feature any color graphics? Will the masters be photocopied or printed via offset printing techniques? Will the publication be folded? Will it be stapled? Stapled where? In a saddle-stitched pattern or by some other method? How will the publication be distributed to the public? By the U.S. Postal Service? With stamps or by bulk-mail permit?

While most of these questions don't apply to WWW pages, similar questions do. Will there be images? In-line or external ones? Will an alternative, text-based option be offered for users with nongraphic browsers? Where will the files for these pages reside? Who will maintain them? Who will assure the continuing validity of the site's links? How will the links be checked? How often will the site be updated?

In either a paper or an electronic format, certain procedures are common. A production schedule should be worked out to ensure the publication is completed on a timely basis. Each task should have a deadline, which should be made clear to all individuals involved. The first element of the schedule is planning. Planning should provide at least a tentative answer to all the questions outlined here, as well as to many others. The publication should be sketched out and put into a design framework. Writing and artwork should be assigned and then completed. Completed materials are then brought into the desktop publishing package and laid out. Original masters of each sheet are then printed to be reproduced and ultimately distributed, or the completed pages are transferred onto the local WWW server.

Another common element to print and electronic publications is a style sheet. The style sheet of a publication makes explicit how repetitive elements will be consistently handled in each part, page, or issue of a publication. Will dates be listed February 7, 1996 or 2/7/96? Will time be 9:00AM, 9AM or 9 o'clock? Is a number displayed as "12" or spelled out as "twelve"? Should articles be written in the third person? In the first person? Are there preferred spellings or capitalizations for certain words ("disk" or "disc," "CD-ROM" or "cd-rom")? These and other similar questions should be spelled out so all the textual elements of a publication will be consistent. A style sheet is helpful even if you are the only writer, because you may not remember how you have handled a like situation in the past. Having to go back and check a small point in a previous publication can be time-consuming and frustrating.

OVERALL GUIDELINES

No matter what the type of publication, the heart of it is the information to be shared, and that information will be conveyed primarily through words, skillfully written words. The writer for any type of informative publication needs to keep certain guidelines in mind:

- *Identify with your audience.* Keep in mind what they want to know and what you need to tell them. Think about how they would like to receive this information, e.g.: Is humor appropriate? Are more examples needed? Should a point of view be taken?
- *Make sure your facts are accurate.* A writer and a publication both rely on the faith of readers to be believe what is written. All care should be exercised to ensure that faith is upheld. Check and doublecheck your facts.
- *Organize your thoughts.* Any publication should have a flow that keeps the audience reading. Each sentence builds on the last to make up a paragraph; each paragraph builds on the last to complete the text.
- *Keep it simple.* You may know a great deal, but don't try to overwhelm the reader by including all of it in any particular publication. Stick to basics. In a newsletter, you probably don't have the space to fully explore a complicated subject; try to stick to the most important 2 or 3 points. In a library guide, a reader is looking for quick instructions on a resource or a compilation of a few of the best research sources. If a WWW page starts to get too long and involved, it needs to be broken up into separate linked pages.
- *Be concise.* This is neither poetry nor the great American novel. The type of writing generally called for in these types of publications is the clean, clear writing of a journalist.
- *Be correct.* Spelling is easily checked, but don't rely solely on automatic spell checkers. You may have spelled a word correctly, but it may not be the word you intended to write. Rules of punctuation also should be adhered to in the interests of the reader.
- *Attract attention.* Journalists may write cleanly, clearly, and concisely; however, they also need to attract the reader's attention and hold it. Writing should be concise and simple, but it should be lively. Some style and per-

sonality are required for someone to want to read your words.

As all journalists know, their writing is subject to editing no matter how clean, clear, and concise it is. The editor must look at the publication as a whole and deal with each part of that whole with new eyes. That is especially difficult if the writer is also the editor, but it is still necessary. There may be space considerations. There may be conflicts of tone between two items of text. There may be any number of reasons for editing and rewriting. An editor must be brutal and a writer not too sensitive. In desktop publishing, where writer and editor often are the same person, this is a neat balancing act.

If you then add in the design and layout responsibilities for the publication, this high-wire act can get very impressive. Or, it can result in a spectacularly bad and ineffective publication. In these pages, we will take a close look at a number of possible approaches that a well-designed publication might take. We will also highlight some of the most important pitfalls to avoid in creating a high-quality publication on your desktop.

SECTION 1

DESKTOP PUBLISHING BASICS

1 PUTTING THE POWER ON YOUR DESKTOP: HARDWARE AND SOFTWARE NEEDS

Desktop publishing presupposes that you have a personal computer (PC) on your desktop and that the computer is loaded with programs enabling you to produce a publication. That computer may be an IBM or IBM clone, or it may be an Apple Macintosh (Mac). Desktop publishing had its beginnings with the Macintosh and the earliest versions of PageMaker, and the Macintosh is ideally suited for desktop publishing because of its easy graphics interface, since emulated by Microsoft Windows. My own background is primarily in a DOS and Windows environment, so that is what I am most familiar with. So bear in mind that the computer environment at your library that will support your desktop publishing project is of little significance to the focus of this book, because the book is about how to plan and perform the desktop publishing function rather than how to use specific software programs written for either Macs or PCs.

THE PERSONAL COMPUTER

A personal computer is made up of five major components: the central processing unit (CPU), the monitor, the keyboard, the mouse, and the printer. In addition, for desktop publishing you may also want to have a scanner and some other peripherals.

The CPU is the brains of the computer. It runs all operations and is categorized by the generation of microprocessor that is plugged into its mother board. All IBM clone microprocessors are descendants of the original "8088/8086" chips in the first PCs. We have since gone through the 286, 386, and 486 generation machines. In the current environment, the Pentium or 586 processor currently holds sway, but the 686 processor is inevitable. The Motorola microprocessors used by the Macintosh are the 68000 series and the PowerPC chip (developed jointly with

IBM). The Performa series of Macs was designed for home use, and the PowerMac for more intensive use.

The capabilities of a system are further categorized by the speed of the processor and the amount of random access memory (RAM) loaded in the unit. RAM is the space allotted by the computer to work on currently loaded programs. Speed is measured in Megahertz (MHz). A minimum of 166MHz is standard, but 180MHz, 200MHz, and more are available as well. As would be expected, the faster a system is the better; but the faster a system is, the more expensive it is. Most personal computers today come with at least 8 megabytes (MB) of RAM, which is ample to run most existing applications. However, 16 (MB) is better for Windows '95 and for future versions of software for both Windows and Macintosh, and so is recommended for a new system—if you can afford it. You can get up to 256 MB of RAM at this point, but you pay a premium.

What if a new personal computer is not in your budget? Can you load desktop publishing software on that old machine that's available? The answer is a qualified yes. For example, I have PageMaker 5 loaded on both the Pentium 120MHz with 16MB RAM in my office at work and on my home PC, which is a 486 33MHz with 8 MB RAM. It runs faster at work, but runs very efficiently at home as well. However, PageMaker version 6.0 is coming out as this is being written. For a PC running Windows 3.1, PageMaker 6.0 calls for 10MB of RAM just to load; under Windows '95, a PC requires a minimum of 8MB RAM. The point is that when new versions of the software are released with new features and new memory requirements, that older machine may be incapable of running the upgrade effectively. In this case, the choice is to continue using the old version of the software, upgrade the old PC's memory, or buy a new PC. The world of computers is one of planned obsolescence with a vengeance.

The next major element of the CPU is the hard drive, which is where programs and data files are stored when not in use. Not surprisingly, the rule of thumb is the bigger the better. The price of storage has dropped remarkably in recent years, so that a hard drive holding a gigabyte (equivalent to 1,000 MB) or more of data is to be expected. As programs become larger and larger, you'll be surprised at how quickly that space is taken up.

A new personal computer also will come with a $3\frac{1}{2}$" floppy disk drive to allow the storage of files on portable "floppy" disks. If you have an older existing IBM PC, it may also have the old-style $5\frac{1}{4}$" floppy drive for the bigger, floppier disks, but that has become largely obsolete technology. A new personal computer is also likely to be a multimedia system that includes an eight-speed

CD-ROM (compact disc-read only memory) drive and speakers. CD-ROM uses optical technology to store extremely large amounts of data. For our purposes, a number of software packages on CD are available that feature images and illustrations that can be imported into your publication. A CD drive is also essential if you will be working with Kodak Photo CDs to bring photographs into your publication. Speakers and a sound card can be useful if you are creating a World Wide Web (WWW) page that includes links to audio files.

All systems also will include a keyboard to enter data and a mouse to navigate the Windows or Macintosh environment. The mouse is the key to the graphic user interface popularized by the Macintosh and emulated by Windows. Its point-and-click method of moving large blocks of text or graphic images or whole files is essential for the layout design process of desktop publishing.

MONITORS

The better the display given by your computer's monitor, the easier it is for you to design and lay out your publication. Pixels are the dots of light that form the image on your screen. The size of a monitor is measured by how many pixels the display is made up of. You will be best off with a Super VGA (SVGA) color display with a pixel resolution of 1024 x 768 or better. For an older machine, you may only have a VGA class display with a pixel resolution of 640 x 480 or 800 x 600. VGA is adequate, but SVGA is sharper and preferable.

The sharpness of the images displayed on your monitor is dependent on the dot pitch—the spacing among the dots. Smaller is better, and dot pitch should be no larger than .28mm. Another major specification for a monitor is its refresh rate, or how quickly the screen is redrawn. The higher the refresh rate, the more stable the image. A refresh rate should be at least 72Hz to prevent flickering.

As for the size of the monitor, a 14" display is barely adequate, and a 17" is very much preferred, but you may pay twice as much for the improved display. The increased size makes a big difference when designing a publication, since the larger the display, the more you see of your page when you are working on its layout. A larger monitor size also permits you to judge better how your page will look when printed. Finally, make sure your video card matches the capabilities of your monitor, particularly if you are upgrading.

PRINTERS

For printed publications, the quality of your printer is of paramount importance. There are many different types of printing technologies: thermal transfer, dot matrix, inkjet, and laser. Of these, the first two are generally inadequate for desktop publishing. Type printed from these technologies is fuzzy and lacks a professional look. Inkjet printers do offer the option of inexpensive color printing and also can provide a fairly good resolution of type. They are excellent printers for most home and office uses, but when you need a professional quality appearance to a document, as you do with desktop publishing, then only a laser printer will do. Generally, a laser printer offers print resolution of 300 dots per inch.

Laser printers work in a similar way to photocopiers. An image of the printed page is laid down by the laser using toner; a photocopier uses a lens essentially to take a picture of the page. What the two have in common is that they work from an image of the entire page. A laser printer does not go line by line, as do the other types of printers, but duplicates the image of the page all at once. While the initial cost of a laser printer will probably be more than even a color inkjet, the per-page expenses are actually less. The quality of the laser printer is measured in its resolution ratio, which is usually either 300 or 600 dots per inch. Laser printers need their own memory, and the rule of thumb is the more the better.

The image is transferred to the printer from the desktop publishing package by the use of a page description language (PDL). A PDL describes every element on a page from characters to graphics to white space and tells the printer where and how it needs to reproduce each element. The leading PDL is PostScript, which is built into most laser printers. For older models, PostScript cartridges could be purchased to load into the printer when printing a PostScript job. If you try to print a PostScript file (like a PageMaker document) on a non-PostScript printer, the result will be pages of computer language instructions. That is because a PostScript file sent to a printer consists of a prologue that defines all of the elements of the output to follow and then a script that details exactly what is to be printed where on the page. PostScript allows text to be presented in a wide range of scalable sizes and styles and for graphics to be printed distinctly in black and white or color (if you have a color laser printer).

PERIPHERALS

A necessary item for any system is a *surge suppressor*, which protects the computer and its data from any sudden electrical increases or decreases. Such surges can come during an electrical storm or from a power outage, and they can "fry" the inner workings of your personal computer or cause stored data to be corrupted.

For desktop publishing, you may also need a *scanner* in order to transfer graphics from a printed page to an electronic file. This is helpful if you want to use a public domain image such as a clip-art illustration, the presidential seal, or a photograph of the library director in your publication. You may even have textual material you need to scan and add to your publication (this is called OCR—optical character recognition). Or perhaps your organization has a distinctive logo to add to your layout. A scanner can transfer any of these paper-based examples to a disk file that can be imported into your publication. No matter what type of image you scan, make sure it is in the public domain or that you have written permission to use the material. Copyright considerations are of the utmost importance when you become a publisher.

Scanners can be hand held, sheet fed, or flatbed. The flatbed is the simplest to operate, most flexible, accurate in its transfers—and expensive. Hand-held scanners are the least expensive and can be useful, but are of a significantly lower quality for two reasons. One, since the hand-held scanner is rolled over the image by the not-always-steady human hand, the quality of the scan can suffer. Two, its scanning width is narrower than that of a flatbed. With a hand-held scanner, larger scans must be done in multiple passes of the scanner and then electronically stitched together. Sheet-fed scanners are at a middle ground, with their own drawbacks. The good news is that prices continue to tumble and quality continues to improve. Flatbed and sheet-fed color scanners can be found for under $500 and hand-held ones for around $200.

There are other options for capturing photographs, but they aren't as flexible in handling other sorts of images; nonphotographic images can't be captured in these ways. One option is a *digital photoprocessing system* like Kodak's Photo CD, in which the photographs you shoot are developed as digital files and transferred to a CD; similar systems use floppy disks to store the digital files. Another option is a digital camera, which takes a photograph and stores it in the memory of the camera; the photographs can then be transferred to your PC as digital files with no external processing. Digital cameras are expensive, however, and their images are of lower quality and resolution than traditional cameras. Images can also be scanned directly from a videotape or videocamera to your computer with the right connections and software. For output, there are special photo printers designed to reproduce photographic-quality prints of digital images.

One last feature to consider for desktop publishing is *Internet access*. For WWW page designers, that is obvious. (Web page designers may need additional hardware and software to handle sound and video files, but those elements won't be addressed here.) But even if you are creating a printed publication, the Internet can be a bountiful source of downloadable images and other materials in the public domain. To get on the Internet, your personal computer needs either a modem or an ethernet card, an account with a network access provider, and the accompanying network graphic browsing software like Netscape or Mosaic. The modem allows you to dial up your Internet access provider using the telephone line. Modems are rated by their baud rate—that is, the transmission speed measured in bits per second. The current standard offering is 14.4 (that's thousands), but 28.8 is recommended, and 56 is coming.

An ethernet card allows your PC to become an actual node on the Internet. It's the best and fastest way to connect to the Internet. Setting up this type of connection is very complicated and is the responsibility of your system's gurus. Talk to them to see if this is possible at your location.

SOFTWARE

Software programs instruct the computer to perform the actions you want it to accomplish. The primary software necessary for desktop publishing is a page-layout program like PageMaker, QuarkXPress, Ventura Publisher, ReadySetGo!, or Publish It!. However, other ancillary programs are recommended as well and are described below.

PAGE-LAYOUT PROGRAMS
A good page-layout program like PageMaker does three things: (1) it allows the user to lay out a page in a multicolumn format; (2) it allows the user to enter or import text in a variety of sizes

and styles; (3) it allows the user to import graphic images from a number of different formats.

Traditionally, pages were laid out along a grid format that permitted multiple columns of varying widths and lengths as well as multicolumn boxes and other features. This was accomplished through a manual paste-up operation for each page of the publication. Some page layout programs are grid-based, but with electronic layout the column is the underlying structure of each page of a publication. The page-layout program lets you select how many columns you want on a page, how wide the columns are, how long they are, and how much space is between columns. It lets you make sure that everything is aligned correctly on the page and lets you see it displayed so on the screen.

Using a page-layout program, text can be imported or entered directly. It can be displayed and printed in a variety of typefaces, type styles, and type sizes. It can be entered anywhere on the page and in different orientations. Spacing between words and lines of text can be freely altered. Guides and rulers can be displayed on the screen and be set up to snap imported elements into alignment in order to ensure that things are laid out precisely and accurately. How a page appears on the screen, aside from guides and rulers, is how the page will appear when printed. The view of a page can be enlarged. Master pages can be set with elements that repeat from page to page, like headers, footers, and page numbers. Style sheets and templates can also be set up.

Graphic elements such as graphs, charts, logos, illustrations, and photos can be imported into the page layout. They can be cropped, enlarged, or shrunken. They can be placed anywhere on a page and then moved, copied, rotated, or reversed. Other graphic elements such as boxes, circles, and rules or lines can be drawn accurately and precisely in a nearly infinite variety of sizes. Graphics can be laid on top of, or underneath, other graphics or text. Shading, shadow effects, and color separation are also possible.

All of these basic things and much more are functions of a good page-layout program like PageMaker. Of course, all of these features do not come cheaply. PageMaker and Ventura Publisher represent the high cost end of page-layout programs. There are also alternatives like Microsoft Publisher, Serif's Page Plus, and PFS Publisher, which have most of the features of the high-end programs at a lower cost and can be excellent solutions for the budget-conscious library. In general, page-layout programs are expensive and require either training or a lot of time reading the manual and talking to other users in order to master the program. Nor do they operate in a vacuum; additional programs are recommended for an optimum setup.

WORD PROCESSING PROGRAMS

First and foremost of those additional programs needed would be a word processing program to enter the text to be imported into the page-layout program. It is generally possible to enter text directly into a page-layout program, but even the best of those programs (PageMaker and Ventura Publisher) lack the breadth of features available from standard word processors. Word processors usually incorporate such tools as a spell checker and a thesaurus as well as such functions as global find-and-replace of specified character strings.

Conversely, basic page layout and graphic image manipulation can be accomplished with the better word processing programs (WordPerfect and Microsoft Word). Using a good word processor like WordPerfect in a WYSIWYG (What You See Is What You Get) Windows or Macintosh environment gives the user a lot of power. This is especially true for a one-column publication. Graphics and figures can be imported; boxes and lines can be drawn; different typefaces can be specified. However, word processing programs are not page-layout programs, so they can only go so far. For the printed publication, both types of programs are recommended.

For a WWW page, the options are different and essentially threefold. WWW pages are based on the Hypertext Markup Language (HTML), which requires the user to "mark up" page text with codes in the HTML computer language. The codes are simple, but this is computer programming at its heart. The three options for marking up your text with HTML codes are: (1) use a word processor and type in both text and coding from scratch; (2) use a word processor with an HTML overlay program and type in the text while adding codes by using certain macro operations keys—even some page-layout programs like PageMaker 6.0 are going in this direction; (3) use a standalone HTML editor to type in text while adding codes by using certain macro operations keys. In any approach, the first requirement is to learn the codes and how to use them. Option 1 requires more keystrokes; options 2 and 3 require learning additional programs.

WWW pages do not import graphics into a text file. Instead the text provides a "link" to a separate image file, generally in either the .jpg or .gif format, and HTML incorporates the image into the same WWW page. The page itself is essentially an ASCII text file. A word processing program is a very good option for a WWW page.

AUXILIARY PROGRAMS

Many other types of programs are likely to be useful to you when creating publications. I list them here to underline the variety of possibilities in this field, not to single out any particular software package.

- A computer drawing program like Corel Draw or a painting program like Microsoft Windows Paintbrush allows you either to create your own images or to alter existing ones.
- Graphics utilities programs can enhance photographs, perform color separation on color graphics, and more.
- File converters convert files from one format to another. You may have downloaded a great .jpg image from the Internet, but are not able to load it into your page-layout program because that program only reads .pcx and .cgm format images. The right file converter will make that .jpg usable to your system.
- Scanners are discussed above, and they need scanning software to transfer print images like clip art to electronic file formats that can then be imported into your page-layout program. While software is usually included with the scanner, commercial scanning software packages may add considerable value to your scanner. You'll probably want software that is able to edit images and handle optical character recognition for text.
- Clip-art collections feature public domain images that can be imported into a publication. There are several such packages available—many with their own retrieval software. There are also many clip-art images available for free or as shareware on the Internet.
- Screen capture programs allow you to download whatever appears on your screen into an electronic file. If you plan on using such a screen dump, though, be careful there are not copyright restrictions on the material.
- Communications software will allow you to gain access to the Internet or electronic bulletin board sites. Out in cyberspace, there are no boundaries, and attractive image files and useful programs are freely available. In particular, you'll need a graphical network browser like Netscape or Mosaic to sample the breadth of colorful choices available easily.
- Files from database and spreadsheet packages can usually be imported into your page-layout software. Graphic elements can be imported also; for example, a pie chart

created from a spreadsheet package might illustrate a newsletter item about the organization's finances.

- Font programs can increase the number of typefaces and/ or type sizes you have to work with for your publication; you may need a variety for body text, headlines, and display text. Thousands of fonts are available commercially, for free, and as shareware. Fonts need to be downloaded to your computer (screen fonts) and to your printer (printer fonts) and will be discussed fully in chapter 3.

A note about programs: The best known of these types of programs are available commercially. As has been noted, alternative shareware programs are also available for those on a tight budget. Shareware programs can be tried out for free. A good source of shareware on the World Wide Web can be found at http://www.shareware.com/. If you like the program, all the programmer asks is that you send in a small registration fee. Shareware will not answer your page-layout need, but fonts, file converters, clip art, and more are plentiful.

2 THE WHOLE PAGE: OVERALL PRINCIPLES DESIGN

Whether your publication will be on paper or on the m̤, the place to start is with the page (or screen): How do you want it to look? Will your intended audience be most receptive to a formal look or a casual one, to a cool image or a warm one, to an open and friendly appearance or a sharp, professional one? The design of your layout needs to address these questions. Decisions on typography and graphic elements will play a large role in the look of your publication as well; they will be discussed in chapters 3 and 4. For this chapter, we will examine the page itself.

The format and size of your page (or screen) will vary according to the type of publication. A printed publication is most often going to use the standard 8½"x 11" page and will be oriented so the page is taller than it is wide—known as portrait style. That is definitely the case with most newsletters, although with the newsletter you must take into consideration the look of two facing pages when you design your page. Some publications use larger or smaller paper sizes, and some use a "landscape" style where the page is wider than it is tall (often used for brochures folded in three sections).

In addition, while most publications may have black ink on white paper, there are other possibilities. Maybe you want the elegant look that gray paper can give. Or maybe the more stylized look of an off-white. If you are having the publication professionally printed, different colors of ink for text or lines or tinted screens are also possible. The only rule of thumb is to make sure that your experimentation in this direction doesn't make the publication unreadable or unappealing. For instance, black text on dark blue paper will be very difficult to read, while some shades of paper like canary yellow may be too garish for the tone of your publication.

The basic features of the printed page include Margins, Body Text, Bylines, Footers, Rules, Headlines, Subheads, and Taglines (see Figure 2.1).

An electronic publication's "page" is the computer screen. Electronic publications need to be oriented to what will fit legibly in

FIGURE 2.1 Elements of the Printed Page

Rule

Alley

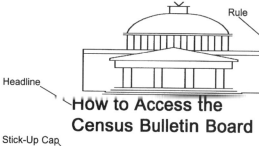

Headline

How to Access the Census Bulletin Board

Stick-Up Cap

Dial (301)763-7554. If you haven't already signed up, you will be prompted to add your name to the system, answer some questions and assign a password.

Left Margin

When you are ready to download and after you have read the bulletins, messages, etc., you must go back to the main menu entitled, "Welcome to the Census Economic Special Interest Group"

- Select o> other special interest groups
- Select 5> CD-Rom Software, data release schedules & related topics
- Select f> go to files transfer menu if you wish to download
- Select c> Census Bureau Download Area (File lists)
- Select 5> Files area #5 ... CD-Rom software and press Return.

Subhead

File Selection

Screen

The system will begin scrolling through a very long list of the files available in that file area. If you already know the name of the file you wish to download, type s to stop the scrolling. A full listing of the files available entitled filelist.txt makes the downloading faster, since you won't have to scroll through many listings.

Body Text

After you have stopped the scrolling, a menu at the bottom of the screen will appear. Select d> download and press return. You will be prompted to enter the filename. Type in the name of the file you wish. Remember you are in area #5 and not every filename is found in that area.

Transfer Protocols

When you type d> download, a menu will appear asking you to select from the following transfer protocols. If using PROCOMM communications software, select x modem

If using PROCOMM, you then need to open PROCOMM up for accepting the transmission. To do this, press the PgDn key. A menu simular to the transfer protocols screen appears. Select xmodem and type your filename such as a:testfile. Press return and that should activate the download. The system will tell you how long the transmission is expected to take.

Byline

When transmission is finished, you may exit the system by selecting g> goodbye.
-- Dxxxxx H. Kxxxxx, University of X

Where the Axe Falls:

Tagline

Excerpts from the 11/18/92 Letter from Wayne Kelley to Depositories

...Reductions in LPS personnel, operations and infrastructure took precedence over reductions in products distributed and services rendered...However, in order to realize the magnitude of savings necessary to stay within the appropriation, LPS was constrained to make changes in formats and types of material available to depository libraries...These reductions included:

Limiting the distribution of Department of Energy microfiche, National Aeronautics and Space Administration microfiche, and the bound Treaties and Other International Acts to regional depositories.

Right Margin

Distributing the U.S. Reports, Official Gazette (patents and trademarks), Army Technical Manuals, House and Senate Calendars, slip treaties, and slip Supreme Court opinions in microfiche only.

Using the new ACSIS (Acquisitions, Classification, and Shipment Information System) database to improve accuracy in placing printing requisitions.... if shortages do occur, LPS will go back-to-press only for certain core publications.

Limiting claims fulfillment services by allowing claims only from regional depositories for microfiche distributed by LPS and by limiting paper claims from all depositories to certain core publications...

Distributing the bound U.S. Congressional Serial Set only to regional depositories, beginning with the 102nd Congress, 1st Session...

Jumpline

Continued on page 8

Steno Pool

Rule

In an introduction to Frances McCue's The Stenographer's Breakfast (Beacon 1992), fellow poet Colleen J. McElroy writes somewhat unenthusiastically about her "early graduate student years...as an assistant to the Government Documents Librarian." "The Documents room was a small space clotted ceiling to floor with pale brown stacks of cardboard boxes, ragged piles of pamphlets, reports and booklets, hundreds of boxes of file cards and bins of letter shelves -- all of it coated with an almost imperceptible layer of dust...My job was to file the mess before it turned to mulch...Each day I coded parcels...under an alphabetic cross-hatch of decimals, dashes and numbers that forced me to think in a language that was completely nonfunctional outside the confines of the Documents room. And all of this while regular library traffic swirled past the door and onto brighter subjects in the seemingly legible languages of law, literature, biology and social subjects.

"If I complained, the Documents librarian would say, "Don't worry. They have to come this way soon. We hold the key to all in this room.""

Footer

the display of most computer monitors. And since computer monitors vary widely in their size, page design for digital pages is an imperfect science. Indeed, many of the basic elements of the printed page such as top and bottom margins, tinted screens, and jumplines have no equivalent on the digital page. Digital pages, in contrast to printed ones, consist generally of a Title (which does not display on the page), Headlines, Subheads, Body Text, Links, Lists, Images, and an Address (an electronic byline) (see Figure 2.2).

DESIGN BY GRID

All publications, particularly printed ones, have an underlying framework or grid. The grid refers to the pattern of vertical and horizontal lines on layout sheets that allow traditional paste-up artists easily to align the text and graphics of a publication precisely and accurately. The grid is based on a unit of measure called the pica, and there are 6 picas to the inch. In desktop publishing, rulers can be displayed on the screen measuring either picas or inches so that lines, margins, and other page features can be drawn according to either unit of measurement.

The grid system divides the page into a system of square and rectangular boxes in order to accommodate the overall design of the page. A well-conceived grid makes page layout easier, because the available space for text and graphics is clear. You only need to decide how those elements fit into your existing grid—along with one more element: white or blank space.

White space is the space found in the margins, between lines of text, between body text and headlines, between text and graphics, between characters, and even within characters. White space is a major factor in keeping your page readable and attractive; it is what keeps your page from looking too cluttered and busy—and readers will avoid cluttered, busy pages. A cluttered page might have too much text, too many graphic elements, or both. White space alleviates the clutter. When used well, white space gives a page an open and readable look. Generally, space between lines should be greater than that between words, and space between words should be greater than that between characters.

Sometimes, pages are simply badly arranged, although they may have a good amount and an even mix of text and graphics. For this problem, the use of lines can be helpful. Lines can define columns, set off graphics, or emphasize words. They can give order

FIGURE 2.2 Elements of the Digital Page

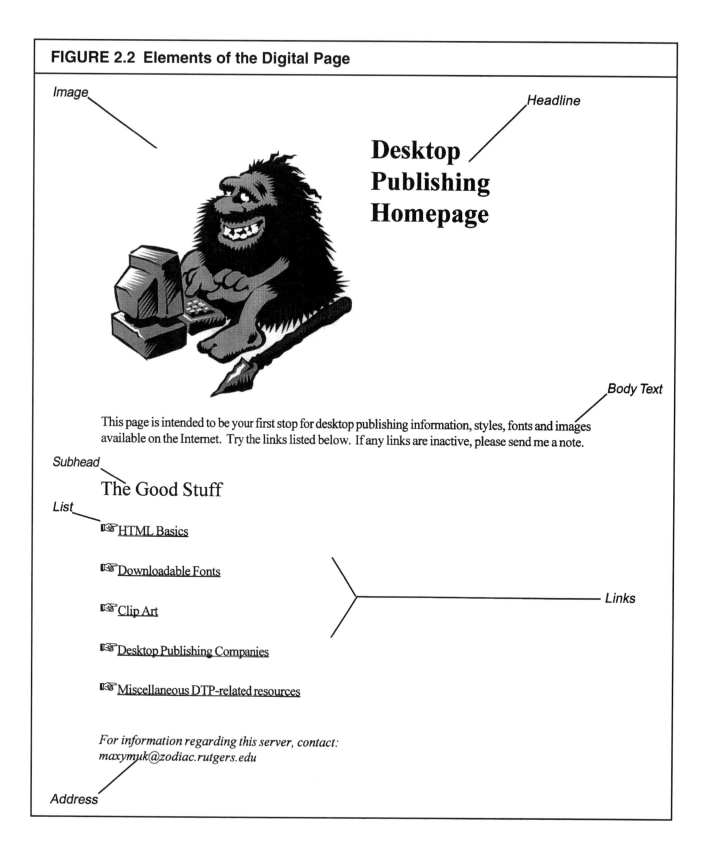

to your page, as can the right amount and arrangement of white space.

Desktop publishing gives you the power to make adjustments in each of these areas.

MARGINS

How wide are your margins? In traditional layout methods, a standard margin, be it top, bottom, right, or left, is 5 picas or $^5/_6$ of an inch. Your desktop publishing program may default to a value of $^3/_4$ of an inch, though. The space between columns of text is generally from 1 to 2 picas. In any case, margins are easily increased or decreased with a desktop publishing program. If you are running any illustrative text or graphics in those margins, you may want to increase their size.

LEADING

The space between lines of text is called leading, so called because, when text was laid out by hand, strips of lead were placed between the rows of text for spacing. You might want to adjust leading if the text appears too tight due to the height of the letters that ascend (like "h") or descend (like "g"). You might also want to increase leading for its overall effect on the look of the page. Leading can also be decreased for spacing considerations, especially for sections of text where all capital letters are used. With all caps, no letters will dip below the line and intrude on the next line, so leading can be tightened.

HEADLINES

Blank space above headlines should be approximately double the space between the headline and the text it accompanies. This spacing accentuates the break from the previous text block and emphasizes the connection to the following text.

GRAPHICS

Graphics should accent the text and make it more appealing and readable. They should not overwhelm it. White space around graphics can give the page a clean look and make the graphic more attractive.

KERNING

Kerning, or tracking, is the space between characters. That space may need to be increased if the letters and other characters appear too condensed to be read easily. With boldface type, for example, characters are darker and heavier with ink, appearing to "soak" up white space. This effect also could be apparent when any number of other typographical effects come into play. You might need to decrease character spacing on occasion, too, if letters appear too spread out.

TYPOGRAPHY

As will be discussed in the next chapter, some typefaces are more condensed than others. Depending on the type of publication and the number of columns in the layout, the text may be unreadable in a particular typeface—the characters seemingly too squeezed together, or even individual characters seemingly too compressed. A change of typeface or of its size or style may be necessary.

Desktop publishing also allows you to decide upon central, recurring design elements and to reuse them easily by setting up template files and styles functions. On a template, you can set up columns, a nameplate, a masthead, graphic placeholders, and other regular features of your publication. With the styles function, you can specify what typeface, size, and attributes you want for the different sorts of text in your publication. Headlines, secondary headlines, body text, captions, bylines, credits, all most likely are assigned distinct sizes or styles in your publication. The styles option is an easy way to access these distinct attributes.

Above all, you need to be consistent in dealing with text, graphics, white space, and the interaction of these elements. If, for example, you change the leading between lines of text on one page, but not on its facing page, this inconsistency will be readily apparent and may be jarring. It is also worth remembering that too much white space does not look good either; it gives the appearance that you have little of interest to say to the reader, that you can't fill your pages. It also creates holes in your page design. Try to strike an attractive balance.

DIGITAL PAGE DESIGN

Digital pages also are a mix of text, graphics, and white space, but the designer has no real control over typographical concerns like typefaces, leading, and kerning. The typeface you use to create a home page, for example, will not necessarily be the typeface in which your readers view that page. That control is given to the user's Internet browser.

This is not to say that you have no control over the ultimate look of your home page, which depends more on how the text and graphics are arranged on the screen and how effectively they are separated by white space or background pattern; you must focus on that which you can control. You can decide whether the background to your page is to be white, a color, or a variety of patterns. You can adjust the color of the text. You can make sure that graphics are the right size and are aligned properly with the text. You can make sure that text is broken up with subheadings and that paragraphs are divided by line breaks. You can make sure that too much information is not jammed onto one page, but is broken up into shorter, more attractive, multiple pages that are logically linked together.

As with printed pages, there should be a unified look to digital pages that should be evident in all the pages of a publication. Similarly, there should be a balance to the grid layout of any type of publication. There may be elements that vary and are asymmetrical, but the overall effect of a page should be harmonious, with all of the parts fitting together well in a particular grid.

CHOOSING A COLUMN GRID

With desktop publishing, grids are described by the number of columns into which a page is divided. The most obvious type of grid is the one-column grid, which features one column of text. Using only one column does not mean that the design has to be dull and uninviting. It can come alive with the placement of graphic elements, the use of subheadlines, breaking up the text with white space, the use of logos, setting the text column off center, and many other possibilities (see Figure 2.3).

The one-column format lends itself very well to WWW pages and to library handouts. It is even a good format for newsy, to-the-point newsletters of either one or two pages that are to be printed on one sheet of paper.

A two-column grid design is used for some WWW pages and library handouts, but is most often used in newsletters. It gives you a more flexible design than the one-column grid and is very easy to work with. The two columns can be either of equal size or asymmetrical. Margins can be wide for an appealing, airy look or they can be narrow for publications with a great deal of running text.

There are two common pitfalls with this grid. First, a two-column page can have too much sameness and symmetry. For example, if both columns on a page are text-filled, have the same beginning and end points, and are not broken up by any graphic elements, then the appearance is very boring. When the headlines on two or more columns are in near perfect alignment, it's called the "tombstone effect" because it gives the page the appearance of a graveyard with the aligned headlines sticking up as tombstones; it is deadly. Second, a two-column grid can be too dense with text. Again, the answer is white space and graphics for a proper mix of visual elements.

FIGURE 2.3 The One-Column Grid

One Column Grid Schematics

Single block of text centered

Off-center single block of text

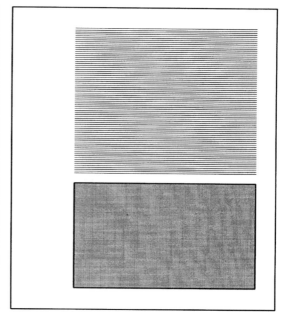

Centered block of text wrapped around a graphic element

Off-center block of text with graphic element filling the entire column

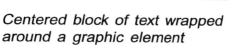

Asymmetrical, two-column grids offer a wide-open look and allow for a dynamic use of the space on the page. The wide column is for text and large graphics; the narrow column is ideal for logos, photos, small graphics, short display text, headlines, captions, and other special elements. See Figure 2.4 for different two-column grid layouts.

The three-column grid is even more flexible and offers an even wider array of possibilities for a newsletter than does the two-column grid (see Figure 2.5). Your columns can be of equal size, or you can have two wide and one narrow or even two narrow and one wide. Headlines, graphics, and pull quotes can range across one, two, or three columns. The sizes of these elements can be varied even within a single page. Text can easily flow from the bottom of one column to the top of the next and be readable.

Increased possibilities mean increased decisions. Using a three-column grid can lead to a greater amount of time spent experimenting with potential layout designs. It can also lead to some very striking layouts. You will have to decide how much flexibility you can manage.

Four- and five-column grids continue the increases in both flexibility and complexity for the layout of newsletters—not to mention the skill level of the designer (see Figure 2.6). All the features of three-column layouts discussed above hold true for four- and five-column grids. Furthermore, four-and five-column grids incorporate the use of sidebars very effectively and make good use of mixed grids, employ columns of variable widths in possible layouts too numerous to count.

Another way to shape a grid-based layout is to echo some of the forms taken by the very letters on a page. L and T are both very popular page designs; O and Z are also not uncommon. An L-shaped layout is very effective at curling around and enclosing the other elements on the page. The L also may be found inverted or flipped on its side. Likewise, the T-shape is often inverted or flipped sideways on a designed page. When the T-shape is inverted, it frequently gives the page the look of a pyramid, attractive and solid. An O-shaped page directs the reader's eye to a point of focus generally in the center of the page and tends to make a page very symmetrical. The Z-shaped page is based on a diagonal orientation and also leads the reader's eyes across a very striking page.

FIGURE 2.4 The Two-Column Grid

Two-Column Grid

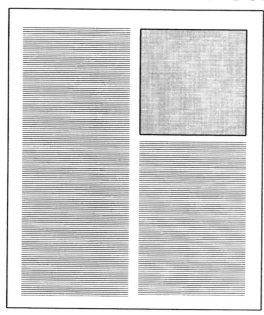

Symmetrical design with graphic in one column

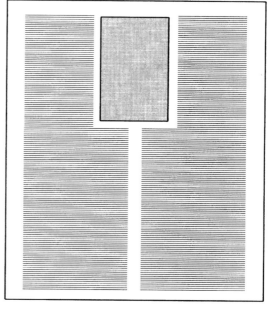

Symmetrical design with graphic overlapping both columns

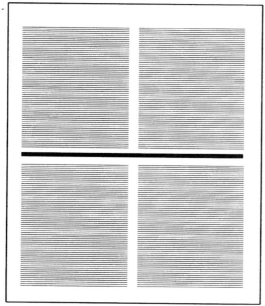

Symmetrical design with horizontal division of page

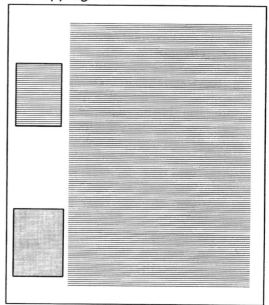

Asymmetrical design with graphic and display text in narrow column

FIGURE 2.5 The Three-Column Grid

Three-Column Grid

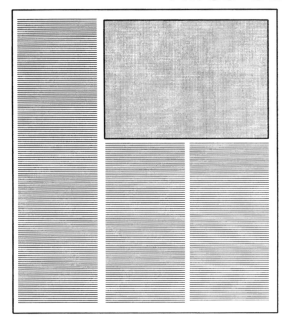

Symmetrical with two-column
graphic

Mix of one and three column with
graphic

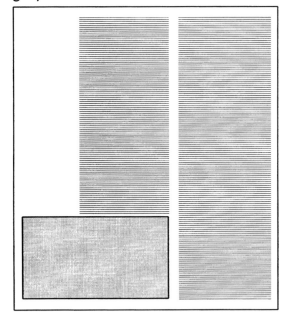

Asymmetrical, one narrow and two
wide, with two-column graphic

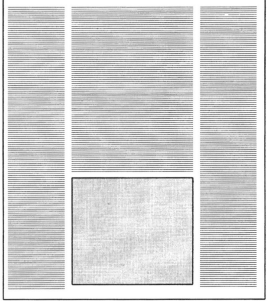

Symmetrical, two narrow and one
wide, with one-column graphic

FIGURE 2.6 Four- and Five-Column Grids

Four- and Five-Column Grids

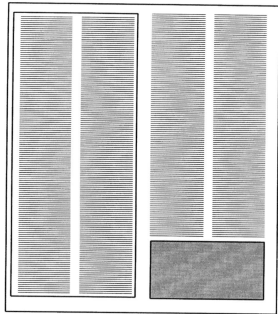

Symmetrical with two-column sidebar and two-column graphic

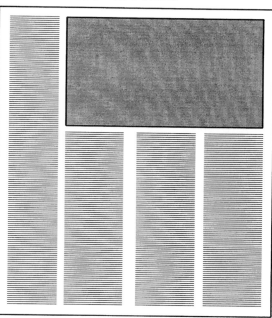

Symmetrical with three-column graphic

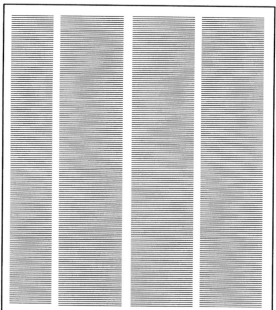

Asymmetrical with one narrow column

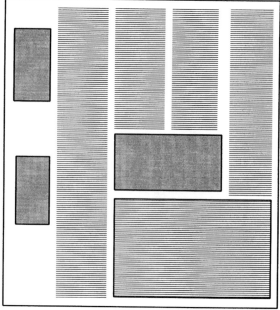

Mixed five column with three-column sidebar and three graphics

CONSIDERATIONS FOR GOOD DESIGN

No matter the layout, all good designs weave together certain common threads. Those threads, which include balance, proportion, focus, and unity, can create an infinite variety of textures and patterns in a publication. The desktop publisher must understand these factors and use them skillfully in the creation of an attractive page. That page should capture a reader's attention, hold it, and help the reader group the information by importance.

Balance is evident in all good design. In a well-designed publication, text, graphics, and white space do not look as if they were just thrown on the page haphazardly, but that they were placed where they belong. All the areas of interest should not be off in one corner of a page. In a symmetrical, centered layout, the right and left hand sides or top and bottom of the page are essentially mirror images of one another. This sameness can get a little monotonous, but it is very easy to work with. An asymmetrical page can, and should, be balanced as well. The right side of the page is still balanced against the left; the top is still weighted optically in relation to the bottom. However, the choices a designer must make are not as obvious. An asymmetrical page appears more spontaneous and effortless, but is actually much more difficult to accomplish.

Proportion poses such questions as: How big is the graphical, textual, or spatial element? How dark is it? Where on the page is it located? Is it in proportion to the elements around it? Is it in proportion to everything else on the page? In short, proportion is achieved through comparison of a part both to the page as a whole and to other parts of the page. A two-column graphic may look modest on a four-column grid, but adding a second, smaller, related graphic can make the first look larger and more dominant. Likewise, the size of type used for a headline is judged in proportion to the size of the page, the number of columns, the length of the story, and the type size for the body text of the item.

Focus brings out related questions: Is the element placed where the focus of the reader is directed? Is the reader then led to another element? To answer these questions, the designer must decide what is the most important information on the page as well as which are the most visually interesting elements. A reader's natural inclination is to read from left to right, starting from the upper left of the page. The most important information on the page should be there unless the page is specifically designed to start the reader elsewhere. In general, readers will focus on large before small, color before black and white, and black before white on a page. Balance, proportion, and focus become evident from the interactions among the separate textual, graphical, and spatial elements on the page. Questions such as those above can only be answered in relative terms by comparing all strands that make up a page.

Unity is how all the elements on a page coalesce and merge into a harmonious, coherent whole. Everything fits together; no single element seems to be screaming, "What am I doing on this page!" There is room for originality and anomaly, but within a recognizable framework. A symmetrical design can help achieve a unified whole, but unity is also found in asymmetrical designs that feature disproportion, contrast, and incongruity.

Graphic artists study the principles of design in great detail as they apprentice their craft over a span of many years. The demands of the library world often short-circuit ideal scenarios. It's very likely that your library director assigns the task of creating a newsletter, a series of handouts, WWW home page, or any number of other types of publications to someone with no background in design—i.e., you. Is this situation fraught with peril? Yes and no.

Yes, there is peril, but it can be sidestepped. Look around at similar publications. Study the ones that look good to you. Rely on your instinctual tendency toward balance, unity, and organization, and keep it simple. Do a mock-up of your page layout and print page proofs to see how your design can be improved. Your first publications may not be as exciting as those you notice in a glossy magazine, but they can still be effective. Remember, there is not just one answer to a design problem, and there is disagreement even among experts on all elements of design. Some favor sans serif type for body text, for example, but others hate that look. Some think a script type adds an informal look to a publication; others think it looks artificial. Trust your judgement, and enjoy the creative process.

3 CHARACTER SKETCH: ESSENTIALS OF TYPOGRAPHY

You've seen type all your life in books, magazines, and brochures, on posters, tax forms, cereal boxes, T-shirts, and many other places. Now let's take a closer look at this defining component of your publication. Type evokes a mood and conveys particular feelings or impressions to the reader. Type accents the meaning of the words it depicts. Type can give a publication a serious face, a casual face, or even a frivolous one. In short, different typefaces have different personalities, and it is important to choose an appropriate one, because the right typeface will enhance the message you are trying to communicate in your publication.

A typeface is a collection of the twenty-six upper-case (capital) and twenty-six lower-case letters of the alphabet, ten numerals, and a variety of punctuation marks designed in a unique style. The term "font" is used interchangeably with typeface.

The appropriate typeface will suit the character of your publication and will be both readable and legible. Readability refers to the ease with which text can be read, legibility to the ease with which characters can be recognized. They are distinct concepts, but work in concert in well-designed publications that use the right typefaces.

BASIC TYPEFACE CHARACTERISTICS

Certain characteristics are common to all typefaces:

- *Ascender* is the stroke of lower-case letters that rises above the x height (see below). Examples of letters with ascenders are h and b.
- *Baseline* is an imaginary line on which all letters sit.
- *Cap height* is the distance from the baseline to the top of a capital letter. Sometimes there is said to be a cap line, that is, an imaginary line at the height of the top of capitals. In some typefaces, the ascenders of lower-case letters extend above the cap line.
- *Counter* is the white space center of enclosed rounded let-

ters like Bb, Dd, Pp. The important thing to keep in mind is that the size of your letters should not be so small that the counter is overwhelmed with black.

- *Descender* is the part of a lower-case letter that dips below the baseline. Good examples are g, p, and y.
- *Serif* is the small finishing stroke of characters in serif typefaces.
- *Stem* is the vertical stroke of any letter.
- *Waist line* is an imaginary line at the x height of lower-case letters.
- *X height* is the distance between the baseline and the top of lower-case letters without ascenders like a, c, and x.

Figure 3.1 demonstrates these features.

Typefaces are distinguished in different ways. In desktop publishing, typefaces are sometimes divided into Type 1–compatible and TrueType-compatible fonts. The same typeface may be available in either format. Type 1 and TrueType refer to the type of printers on which they can be printed. Type 1 was developed by Adobe, which also developed the PostScript printing language. Type 1 fonts are designed for PostScript printers. TrueType was developed by Apple and Microsoft and can be printed on True-Image printers and PostScript ones as well.

A more traditional and useful way to distinguish typefaces is according to their style. Typographers might divide typefaces into several groups including Romans, Transitionals, Lineals, and Glyphs according to criteria arcane to the novice. For our pur-

FIGURE 3.1 Typeface Terminology

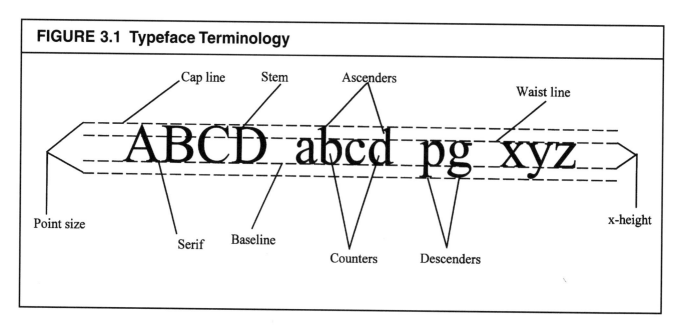

poses, we can use the common shorthand approach of serifs, sans serifs, and scripts.

Serif type is very traditional and is what you see in most books and magazines in the United States. Characters in serif type feature a small finishing stroke or serif, which creates a natural spacing for this group of typefaces, helping to make serif type very readable. Serif typefaces are used for body text in this country because of that readability. There have been studies indicating that serif text is more easily read than sans serif. It has been speculated that the serif helps to guide the reader's eye to the next letter. However, it has also been speculated that serif text is found to be more readable simply because it is more familiar. In Europe, sans serif type is generally used for body text. Examples of serif type include Times New Roman, Garmond, Bookman Old Style, and Perpetua (see Figure 3.2).

Sans serif, then, is type where the characters have no serif, or finishing stroke. (Sans is French for "without.") Sans serif text has a very clean, clinical, and modern look, although the oldest sans serif typefaces date back to the nineteenth century. This type is often used very effectively for headlines in this country. Examples include Helvetica, Century Gothic, Univers, and Impact (see Figure 3.3).

Script typefaces attempt to simulate cursive handwriting by giving the appearance of each character connecting to the next. Some ascribe a casual personality to script typefaces, others find its appearance artificial, as if the user were trying too hard to appear to be friendly. These typefaces tend to be more difficult to read and should be used sparingly, if at all, and only for effect. Examples include Brush Script, Matura Script Capitals, and Coronet (see Figure 3.4).

One final class of typefaces to mention is the *symbolic group*. Typefaces like Zapf Dingbats and Wingdings include special characters and symbols that can greatly enhance a page (see Figure 3.5).

OTHER TYPEFACE CHARACTERISTICS

No matter which of these groups a typeface fits, additional qualities help determine its personality. The most significant of these qualities are size, style, and weight. A typeface family is made up of a particular typeface with all its different sizes, styles, and weights.

FIGURE 3.2 Some Serif Typefaces

Serif

Times New Roman
ABCDEFGHIJKLMNOPQRSTUVWXYZ
abcdefghijklmnopqrstuvwxyz
1234567890!@#$%^&*)(:;",.?

Garmond
ABCDEFGHIJKLMNOPQRSTUVWXYZ
abcdefghijklmnopqrstuvwxyz
1234567890!@#$%^&*)(:;",.?

Bookman Old Style
ABCDEFGHIJKLMNOPQRSTUVWXYZ
abcdefghijklmnopqrstuvwxyz
1234567890!@#$%^&*)(:;",.?

Perpetua
ABCDEFGHIJKLMNOPQRSTUVWXYZ
abcdefghijklmnopqrstuvwxyz
1234567890!@#$%^&*)(:;",.?

TYPE SIZES

The size of type is measured in points. There are 72 points to the inch. For example, in a 72-point headline the characters will be roughly one inch tall. Typefaces commonly come in 6, 7, 8, 9, 10, 11, 12, 14, 18, 24, 30, 36, 48, 60, and 72 point sizes (see Figure 3.6). The beauty of desktop publishing is that type size is

---

FIGURE 3.3 Some Sans Serif Typefaces

Sans Serif

Helvetica
ABCDEFGHIJKLMNOPQRSTUVWXYZ
abcdefghijklmnopqrstuvwxyz
1234567890!@#$%^&*)(:;",.?

Century Gothic
ABCDEFGHIJKLMNOPQRSTUVWXYZ
abcdefghijklmnopqrstuvwxyz
1234567890!@#$%^&*)(:;",.?

Univers
ABCDEFGHIJKLMNOPQRSTUVWXYZ
abcdefghijklmnopqrstuvwxyz
1234567890!@#$%^&*)(:;",.?

Impact
ABCDEFGHIJKLMNOPQRSTUVWXYZ
abcdefghijklmnopqrstuvwxyz
1234567890!@#$%^&*)(:;",.?

---

scalable. If you want 17-point type rather than the more standard 18, you can make that adjustment easily. Scalable type is then printed accurately by PostScript printers. Body text of most publications is set in 8 to 12 point type, most likely 10 to 12. Display text such as a headline is set in 14 point and above. Subheads are usually 14 or 18 point, and main headlines 24 point and up.

FIGURE 3.4 Some Script Typefaces

Script

Brush Script

ABCDEFGHIJKLMNOPQRSTUVWXYZ

abcdefghijklmnopqrstuvwxyz

1234567890!@#$%^&)(:;",.?*

Matura Script Capitals

ABCDEFGHIJKLMNOPQRSTUVWXYZ

abcdefghijklmnopqrstuvwxyz

1234567890!@#$%^&)(:;",.?*

Coronet

ABCDEFGHIJKLMNOPQRSTUVWXYZ

abcdefghijklmnopqrstuvwxyz

1234567890!@#$%^&)(:;",.?*

TYPE STYLES

Style can refer to two things. One way to look at the style of a particular typeface as a whole is that it can be considered normal, condensed, or expanded. As you would guess, condensed typefaces condense the space between characters, while expanded typefaces expand them.

The style of type, however, also can refer to stylistic effects that can be applied to any typeface. In this case, style means normal, italic, bold, bold italic, underlined, outlined, shadowed, or reversed (see Figure 3.7). Aside from normal, all of these styles are essentially special effects, which should be used sparingly. If used too much, they become less than special and tougher to read. Underlining in particular should be avoided in most cases. It is a holdover from the typewriter era and is substantially more difficult to read.

FIGURE 3.5 Some Symbolic Typefaces

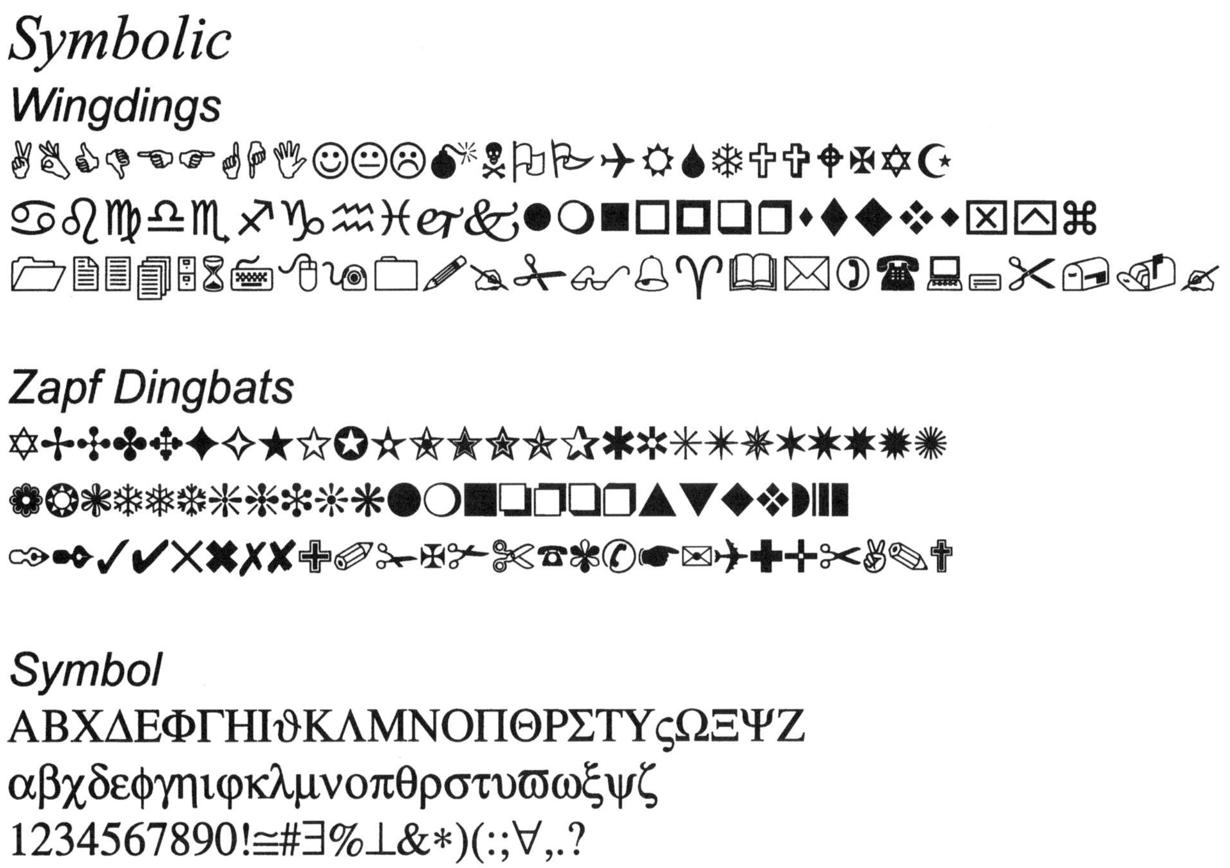

Symbolic

Wingdings

✌✋👌👈👉☝👆👇✊✋☺😐☹💣✹☠🏳🏴✈☼💧❄✝✞✠✡✨☪

♋♌♍♎♏♐♑♒♓⌘❦❧◦●○■□▢▣▤◆◇◈❖◆⊠△⌘

📁📑📄📑📇⌛⌨🖱💼✏✎✐✂✄✁🔔♈📖📧🌙📞💻▭✂📬📪📫🖋

Zapf Dingbats

✡✜✣✤✥✦✧★☆✪✰✱✲✳✴✵✶✷✸✺✻✼✽✾✿❀

❁❂❃❄❅❆❇❈❉❊❋●○❏□❐❑❒▲▼◆❖❱❚❙❘

✎✏✑✓✔✕✖✗✘✚✐✂✁✂✃❀✆✝☎✈✠✜✛❁✌🖉🖋✝

Symbol

ΑΒΧΔΕΦΓΗΙϑΚΛΜΝΟΠΘΡΣΤΥςΩΞΨΖ
αβχδεφγηιφκλμνοπθρστυϖωξψζ
1234567890!≅#∃%⊥&*)(:;∀,.?

TYPE WEIGHTS

The weight of type is determined by the amount of ink a typeface uses. The darker the characters appear on the page, the heavier the type. It is most obvious when you are using boldface or italic type because boldface adds to the blackness of the characters and is very heavy; italic decreases that blackness and is very light (see Figure 3.8). However, there are significant variations in the weight of different typefaces themselves. Two typefaces of the same size and style can carry vastly different weights on a given page.

FIGURE 3.6 Point Size of Type

Times Roman 6 Point type
Times Roman 7 Point type
Times Roman 8 Point type
Times Roman 9 Point type
Times Roman 10 Point type
Times Roman 11 Point type
Times Roman 12 Point type
Times Roman 14 Point type
Times Roman 18 Point type
Times Roman 24 Point type
Times Roman 30 Point type
Times Roman 36 Point type
Times Roman 48 Point type
Times Roman 60 Point type
Times Roman 72 Point type

FIGURE 3.7 Type Styles

Times Roman Normal

Times Roman Bold

Times Roman Italic

Times Roman Bold Italic

Times Roman Underlined

Times Roman Reversed

ADDITIONAL REFINEMENTS

There are a number of additional methods that affect the look of the text on a page. Again, in a traditional typesetting operation, these involved skills that one mastered over a long period of time. With desktop publishing, they are at the disposal of both novices and experienced layout artists. In most cases, you can rely on the automatic settings of your page-layout program for these concerns.

LEADING

Leading was discussed in the last chapter, and is the space between lines of text. As a general rule, leading should be 120 percent of the point size of the type. If you are using 10-point type, then leading should be 12 point. Often, type will be described as being 10/12 or 11/13. The dual number is giving you both the type size and the leading size (or actually, the type size plus the leading comprises the second number). If leading is the same as point size, 10/10 for example, the descenders of line 1 will bump

FIGURE 3.8 Type Weights

The weight of a typeface depends on how heavy the text appears, on how much ink the characters appear to soak up, on how dark the text makes the page look, on how much white space is visible within the letters. These examples are all set in 11 point ragged right text, but are different typefaces. Some are clearly heavier than others. The weight of a text helps give the type its personality.

Times New Roman

The weight of a typeface depends on how heavy the text appears, on how much ink the characters appear to soak up, on how dark the text makes the page look, on how much white space is visible within the letters. These examples are all set in 11 point ragged right text, but are different typefaces. Some are clearly heavier than others. The weight of a text helps give the type its personality.

Garmond

The weight of a typeface depends on how heavy the text appears, on how much ink the characters appear to soak up, on how dark the text makes the page look, on how much white space is visible within the letters. These examples are all set in 11 point ragged right text, but are different typefaces. Some are clearly heavier than others. The weight of a text helps give the type its personality.

Bookman Old Style

The weight of a typeface depends on how heavy the text appears, on how much ink the characters appear to soak up, on how dark the text makes the page look, on how much white space is visible within the letters. These examples are all set in 11 point ragged right text, but are different typefaces. Some are clearly heavier than others. The weight of a text helps give the type its personality.

Helvetica

The weight of a typeface depends on how heavy the text appears, on how much ink the characters appear to soak up, on how dark the text makes the page look, on how much white space is visible within the letters. These examples are all set in 11 point ragged right text, but are different typefaces. Some are clearly heavier than others. The weight of a text helps give the type its personality.

Univers

The weight of a typeface depends on how heavy the text appears, on how much ink the characters appear to soak up, on how dark the text makes the page look, on how much white space is visible within the letters. These examples are all set in 11 point ragged right text, but are different typefaces. Some are clearly heavier than others. The weight of a text helps give the type its personality.

Impact

into the cap line of line 2. One can even set leading to be smaller than the point size of the type, allowing the cap line of the second line to intrude on the descenders from the first line. The rare occasion in which this would come into play would be for headlines set in all caps that you want displayed very tightly. But this is usually not advisable because the result is very hard to read.

KERNING (TRACKING)

A second alteration, also discussed in the last chapter, is kerning, or tracking, which is an additional feature in page-layout programs. Kerning tightens the space between characters (see Figure 3.9). Again, you will want to diverge from the automatic settings only in rare instances. Headlines are probably the only text you will want kerned, because the type is larger and thus the space between characters is larger and more noticeable. Kerning works with pairs of characters. Your page-layout program can be set automatically to kern any characters above a specified point size, 18 for example.

LINE LENGTH

Another consideration is line length, which will depend on two things: the number of columns in your page layout and the point size of your type. There are a number of formulas to determine line length, but the easiest is to double your point size to get the appropriate length of line in picas. Remember, there are 6 picas to the inch. So for a two-column layout using 11-point type, each column should allow for a 22-pica line length (slightly more than $3^{1}/_{2}$"). The rule of thumb is larger point sizes need larger line lengths to be most readable, and smaller point sizes need shorter line lengths to be most readable.

ALIGNMENT

One final refinement is how the text is aligned on the page. Text can be aligned flush left/ragged right, where the copy begins flush to the left-hand side of the column, and the ends of the lines are uneven or ragged. Text can be centered, where each line has equal space on both the right and the left. Text can be aligned flush right/ragged left as well, which has characteristics the opposite of ragged-right text. Or, text can be justified, in which both the beginning and end of each line is flush with the column, i.e., all line endings are even.

Essentially there are two choices here: ragged right or justified. Ragged left is used sometimes in captions and credits or for special effect. However, for a culture that reads left to right, ragged

---

FIGURE 3.9 Kerning

KERNED HEADLINE

WAVY GRAVY IS NOT TASTY

UNKERNED HEADLINE

WAVY GRAVY IS NOT TASTY

---

left is harder to read. The reader's eyes have to repeatedly search for the beginning of each line. Centered text is used for some headlines and for occasional special effects, but again is usually harder to read for reasons similar to those regarding ragged left.

Ragged right has a more informal feel and is easy to read since the beginning of each line is the same. The ragged line endings have the advantage of maintaining equal spacing between words because there is no compunction to alter the spacing to make the line ends even. The disadvantage is that it looks ragged and may be interpreted as being less serious.

Justified text has a very serious, formal look and is used in books, newspapers, and magazines because of that. Or, perhaps it appears more serious because it is what is displayed familiarly in serious reading materials. There are problems with justified text, though. One thing to be careful of are wide rivers of white space flowing through the text column due to the uneven distribution of word spacing on the line. If left uncorrected, these rivers can be very distracting to the reader. Another thing to consider here is the use of hyphenation. Hyphenation is essential with justified text, but if hyphens proliferate too greatly, they too, become intrusive to the reader. The shorter the text column, the more likely there will be problems with white space rivers and too many hyphens. Justification gives a page an ordered appearance, but features less white space than ragged right. Either can be used effectively in a publication.

FIGURE 3.10 Line Length, Point Size, and Alignment

The shorter the line length of a column, the smaller the point size of the type. A point size of 12 is probably too big for this column, but 9 point looks good and is more readable.

The shorter the line length of a column, the smaller the point size of the type. A point size of 12 is probably too big for this column, but 9 point looks good and is more readable.

The shorter the line length of a column, the smaller the point size of the type. A point size of 9 is probably too small for this column, but 12 point looks good and is more readable.

The shorter the line length of a column, the smaller the point size of the type. A point size of 9 is probably too small for this column, but 12 point looks good and is more readable.

9 Point Ragged Right   *9 Point Justified*   *12 point Ragged Right*   *12 Point Justified*

Using any alignment style, body text usually should be from 10 to 12 points with 2 points of leading, and should maintain one serif typeface for the entire publication. Paragraphs should be clearly defined by either indenting or using spacing with block paragraphs. As a general rule, ragged right works best with block paragraphs and justified text works best with indented paragraphs. Typefaces should not be wantonly matched throughout a publication. One typeface for body text should be selected and used exclusively, with only rare exceptions. The frivolous use of many typefaces, particularly for body text, takes away from the appearance of the page and the meaning of the information conveyed.

TOOLS FOR TYPOGRAPHIC EMPHASIS

Within the framework of the single typeface, special effects can be indicated with boldface and italic type, pull quotes, and large initial capitals. *Pull quotes* are interesting quotations extracted from the text that are chosen to pull in the reader's attention. Pull quotes are set in display copy sizes and are often offset by lines to further attract the reader. *Large initial capitals* are of two varieties. A stick-up cap is an initial capital letter in a paragraph that is set in a significantly larger point size than the rest of the text and that rises above the line. A drop cap is an initial capital letter in a paragraph that is set in a significantly larger point size than the rest of the text and that drops below the line, with the rest of the text wrapping around it. Make sure that there is enough text in your opening paragraph to extend below the drop cap. Furthermore, a drop cap should begin a word of more than three letters, otherwise the reader may have trouble identifying the word. Both varieties help draw the reader into a story and can be further offset from the body text by employing a different typeface or type style from that of the text.

Like initial caps, *display text* is intended to contrast typographically with body text. Display text is made up of headlines, subheads, captions, credits, and more. It can be larger or smaller than body text, be centered or run ragged left, use all caps or upper/lowercase. It may be in a different typeface and even a different typeface style than body text.

Headlines are meant to be big and bold; they should carry a lot of weight on a page. To accompany most body text, headlines should be 24 point or larger and should have more white space above them than below them. They may be centered and set in all caps, but are usually more striking and readable when they are aligned flush left and are a mix of upper and lower case. It is not even necessary to capitalize the first letter of each word in the headline. The most important words are the ones that need to be capitalized. Headlines set in all capitals appear to be screaming at the reader, and for that reason should be used with restraint. Headlines are often set in a sans serif typeface to further contrast with the body text. *Subheads* will usually follow along in all of these qualities except that they are a smaller size, usually 14–18 point.

Watch out for where headlines and subheads appear on the page. If they are buried near the bottom of the page with only a line or two of text beneath them, the page has an off-balance, distracting look. Also, be careful of where the line breaks fall within your headlines; they should not only look good, but be true to the meaning of the words as well. Don't break a headline at a place that disturbs the message.

Captions and *credits* are meant to contrast with body text. They are usually in a smaller point size and utilize italics, boldface, or boldface italics. They are sometimes aligned ragged left and can be in a different typeface. Because they use a smaller typeface, be careful that the line length is shorter than that of the text column. Otherwise, captions or credits can be difficult to read. *Bylines*, whether they come before or after a story, can use a different typeface as well. However, like body text, display text should be consistent. One or two typefaces should be used for headlines, subheads, captions, credits, and bylines. A publication should not look like a typeface flea market.

Finally, whether we are discussing, typefaces, type styles, type sizes, or a variety of special typographic effects, the idea is the same: don't overdo it. Less is more. Think less about how many neat flashy things you can do and more about what looks best in trying to convey your message. As I've said before, keep it simple.

Final Typography Considerations

Remember that this is a digital environment. Use the tools that are available. Don't use the spacebar to align text; use tabs and indents. Use onscreen guides and rulers. And only one space is needed after a period.

When using acronyms or initials in your text, you should consider using small caps as opposed to regular sized capitals. Small caps are approximately the size of the x height of the typeface. They make the acronyms stand out less from the rest of the text and are more easily read than are regular capitals.

Watch for widows and orphans. Described in a variety of ways by different sources, I define them this way: A widow is a short line (less than a third of a line) at the end of a paragraph that is carried over to a new column or page so it appears as single line of text at the top of a column. An orphan is the opposite case—a single first line of a paragraph stranded at the end of a column. The rest of the paragraph is continued in the next column or on another page. Orphans and widows are universally disliked, because they give a page an off-kilter look and break up the continuity of the text for the reader.

Choose the typeface that is most appropriate to the tone and message you are trying to convey. Don't use a light, laidback-looking typeface if you are trying to convey urgent information. And don't use a heavy, serious-looking face for a flyer for the office Christmas party unless irony is your intention. The size of your page will have bearing here as well. Two extreme examples are that a light typeface will look skimpy on a large page with wide borders, while a heavy typeface will look cramped on a small page that is filled with text.

Avoid the most common typefaces: Times Roman for serif and Helvetica for sans serif. They are both very nice and very popular, but we all see them everywhere. Times Roman does feature slim character stems, which are ideal for narrow newsletter columns, but there are other choices. If you are drawn to them, try to substitute a similar,

4 FINISHING TOUCHES: USING GRAPHICS

The final pieces needed to complete your publication are the graphic or visual elements. These visuals come in a variety of shapes, sizes, and styles. You may want to use any number of combinations of photographs, illustrations, cartoons, maps, diagrams, charts, tables, boxes, tinted screens, or lines. There are important considerations involved in using each of these elements, but certain elements are common to all formats.

Each visual can serve many meaningful functions:

- It can attract attention to the accompanying text. A well-chosen photograph or illustration can often draw the reader's attention to a page.
- It can amplify the message of the text by providing additional information or by presenting information more clearly. A diagram might provide supplementary information or indicate a step-by-step process, and a table might present certain data in a style more fathomable to the audience.
- It can provide relief from columns of unbroken text. An unremitting stream of text is not inviting to a reader's eye.
- It can help establish the mood and style of your publication. Each chosen visual will convey both information and tone to a reader. Tone is important and should not be ignored. Among other things, a visual can help indicate that a publication is a serious one, a friendly one, or a frivolous one.

Conversely, visuals can undermine what you're aiming for. Choose carefully. Visuals selected should be the best ones available and should be clear. Don't use a poor visual just because you feel a page needs "something"; find a better visual or don't use one at all. If the visual is hampered by distracting elements, crop them out. Only the most significant elements should remain in the visual.

Selected visuals should fit into the overall design of your publication. They need to be aligned well with the text and with other graphic elements. There should not be too many of them for the layout, nor should there be too few. When visuals do not fit into the overall design, they can make the page look like a mess.

PHOTOGRAPHS

Photographs probably add more to a publication than any other graphic element, but they are expensive, and working with them can be complicated so they may not fit into your financial or temporal budgets. Obviously, your first consideration is a good image. The photograph itself may be from a staff photographer, a public relations release, or from your own camera. What you need to do is digitize the image into an electronic file.

There are essentially two options for digitizing images and both utilize scanning technology: using a scanner or using a digital photoprocessing system (the origin of which is Kodak's Photo CD). Scanners, like most pieces of electronic technology, continue to improve and come down in price. You can get a flatbed scanner, in which you lay the image on the flat glass bed for scanning. You can also get a less expensive hand-held scanner that you actually roll over the image you want to scan. Good scanners are still expensive and still require an investment of time at startup in learning how best to work them to produce accurate digital reproductions of existing paper images.

Whether it be halftone, grayscale, or color scanning, getting the resolution and quality right is an art. Black-and-white halftone images are **composed entirely** of black dots. The number of black dots printed on the page or displayed on the monitor is varied in order to simulate the shades of gray necessary for a photograph. They can be printed with some success on either an inkjet or laser printer. Grayscale images are made up of dots in a variety of intensities of black—usually either **16 or 256** shades (or more depending on computer memory, hardware, and software limitations). Grayscale images can be edited with much greater control than halftones; you are able to adjust the quality of the image and not just its size, shape, and orientation. Grayscales can be printed by a laser printer or by a professional printer for best effect. Color images usually feature 16, 256, or more shades of color and are more flexible, complicated, and expensive to work with. To print them, you need either to use a color laser printer or to take the image file directly to a professional printer. Of course, you don't have to own or even have access to a scanner to incorporate scanned images into your work. There are service bureaus that you can contract with to digitize your images. Your budget is the main factor here.

By contrast, in a digital photoprocessing system, you shoot your role of film with your camera and send it to a photo CD processing center. For example, Kodak Photo CD is a proprietary system; only Kodak dealers will develop the film and scan the results onto a compact disk, where the images are in a digital format. You will need to have a CD drive capable of reading the digital photo system's CDs and also will need the viewing software used by that system. Once developed, these electronic images can be imported into your page-layout program or into a graphics package like Photoshop or Corel Draw and manipulated in a variety of ways. In a graphics package, images can be altered, cropped, reduced, or enlarged, and their colors can be adjusted. You can similarly manipulate images in your page-layout program, but to a lesser degree. Printing, particularly of color photographs (which will need color separation), can be complicated. Color output formats (the three-part RGB—red green blue; or the four-part CMYK—cyan magenta yellow black) vary depending on the requirements of the hardware producing the final product.

One new option that is decreasing in price is the digital camera; hand-held, like a regular camera, the photographs you take are transformed into computer bytes rather than exposed on film. Your "photographs" can be transferred directly to your PC as a graphics file; there is no photoprocessing. The catch is that the least expensive grayscale digital cameras run close to $400; color ones are at least $800; and professional quality digital cameras can run to several thousand dollars. Ultimately, for all but the most experienced desktop publishers, any method of working with photographs will probably necessitate the involvement of a professional printer or a service bureau for at least one of the steps entailed.

If you are willing to work out the details necessary for using photographs in your publication, however, good ones can add real vitality to your pages. Good photographs are in focus, composed so that the elements in the image are properly balanced and emphasized, and use colors and/or contrast sharply. A good photo should accentuate or complement the subject of the text, and should be reproduced large enough so the reader can easily make out the subject of the image. Be selective, and use only your best shots, the ones that best enhance your page.

Unfortunately, the most common photographs used in newsletters are close-up head ("mug") shots, large posed group shots of committees or staff, and posed shots of a person receiving an award or presentation. All three types are dull, uninteresting, and overused. They add very little to a page. Try to avoid these tired poses, but if you must use them, try to spice them up. Close-up, closely cropped shots are better than distant ones, and an active, off guard, candid subject is superior to a static handshake shot. Use some creativity in composing the photograph.

ILLUSTRATIONS

Generally, illustrations do not add as much life to a page as good photographs do, but they can be much easier to work with and are usually much less expensive. Black-and-white illustrations can either be line drawings, which include no gradations of gray, or grayscale or halftone illustrations that utilize gradations of gray in order to achieve a continuous, overall tone like photographs. Illustrations for desktop publishing can be divided into three categories: (1) hand-drawn art subsequently scanned into a digital image; (2) computer art created by the desktop publisher in a PC paint or draw program; (3) clip art drawn by commercial services and sold on a floppy disk or compact disk.

For hand-drawn art, the concerns of the desktop publisher are similar to those encountered when working with photographs. First, you have to find a good image, draw a good image, or contract with an illustrator to draw a good image. Then you have to wrestle with either a scanner or a service bureau to transform the paper image into digital form.

With self-created computer art, you need the time and artistic skill to work with either a PC paint or draw program. Paint and draw programs are vastly different from one another. Paint programs like MacPaint or Microsoft Paintbrush are used to create bitmapped images. Bitmapped images are constructed of tiny, square dots along a matrix-like grid. When enlarged, a bitmapped image will reveal a jagged edge along any curve (see Figure 4.1). Because of this ragged appearance, bitmapped images should not be enlarged; indeed, they have the highest quality when the original artwork is large so that it can be scaled down if necessary.

Draw programs like MacDraw or Adobe Illustrator are object-oriented illustration programs that utilize vector graphics (see Figure 4.2). The results are also called PostScript art. With draw programs, a curved line is not made up of tiny, square dots strategically aligned, but of an actual curved line. Curved lines are smooth in object-oriented illustrations, and they can be enlarged to any degree without image degradation.

Category three is for those of us who have no particular artistic talent for drawing with pen or mouse, no budget for illustrators, and no time to create simple or elaborate computer illustrations. Clip art is computer-generated art that has already been created by a commercial service and is available relatively inexpensively in electronic form. The quality of images varies, and you may search through picture indexes without finding ex-

FIGURE 4.1 Bitmapped Graphic

Bitmapped Graphic

FIGURE 4.2 Vector Graphic

actly the illustration you want, but clip art is a very useful component for the desktop publisher. As with self-created computer art, the images can either be bitmapped or PostScript. PostScript images are far preferable because they look more attractive and because they are so flexible in their utility. You can enlarge or reduce them to almost any degree, and, as long as you have kept the proportions of the image the same, they still look great. Often, they can be "ungrouped" (one graphic broken into the separate image elements that comprise the whole) or "grouped" and used in conjunction with one another to good effect.

You can easily determine whether you have a bitmapped image or a vector graphic by observing the file-name extension for the image. Common bitmapped image file extensions are .BMP (Windows Bitmap), .PCX (PC Paintbrush), and .TIF (Tagged Image File Format). Common vector graphics file formats are .CGM (Computer Graphics Metafile), .EPS (Encapsulated PostScript File), and .WMF (Windows Metafile). There are many other graphics file formats available like .WPG (WordPerfect Graphics) or .PCD (Kodak Photo CD), so it's important to know which file formats your page-layout program will accept. If you want to use a file format that your page-layout program does not accept, there are a number of file viewers and converters available as shareware or freeware such as LView or WinJPEG that will transform a file from one format to another.

Digital pages routinely use other file formats. The images that appear on a WWW page, whether in-line or external, are usually either .GIF or .JPG files (commonly called GIFs and JPEGs). GIF files are Graphic Interchange Format images, which display with high quality and high resolution, particularly if line drawings or simple photographs. JPG files are Joint Photographic Experts Group (JPEG) images, whose technology encompasses a compression mechanism so that .JPG files are much smaller and take up less disk space and can be downloaded much more quickly than .GIFs. JPEG images also display well and are ideally suited to color photography and artwork.

Another format seen fairly often on the Web is Adobe Acrobat .PDF (Portable Document Format). This format is used extensively by the government and is usually used to mount printed pages on an electronic platform for viewing on a computer in exactly the same format as the printed page. PDF files are essentially scanned images of printed pages.

No matter what the file format and no matter whether the publication is digital or printed, certain guidelines should be followed for all illustrations:

- They should be attractive and/or striking.
- They should be placed comfortably on the page.
- They should augment the text and not overwhelm it.
- They should complement the personality of the publication.
- They should be well-chosen and used sparingly.

CARTOONS

One type of illustration that needs some additional clarification is the cartoon. Humorous, relevant cartoons can add flavor to a publication, but they need to be funny or at least amusing and have some relation to the subject matter of the publication as a whole. If not, they can turn a reader off as being inappropriate or frivolous. Humor is very tricky, and you need to know your audience well to use it effectively. Avoid cartoons that could in any way be interpreted as being offensive, sexist, or controversial, unless that is your aim. The emphasis in this caveat is on "in any way." Some parts of your audience may be very sensitive about certain subjects.

Sources for cartoons include all those discussed in the section on illustrations. Again, for those of us with no artistic talent, clip art can be very useful. Perhaps you'll find an illustration that fits into the mood of your publication and for which you can supply a funny caption. But with clip art, particularly PostScript clip art, you can seamlessly combine more than one visual image into one. Figures 4.3–4.6 demonstrate how disparate images of three different dinosaurs and a prehistoric background scene can be grouped to good effect.

Adding a caption (Figure 4.7) gives you a cartoon to fit into any library publication dealing with the brave new world of the Internet.

MAPS, DIAGRAMS, CHARTS, AND TABLES

Maps, diagrams, charts, and tables are illustrations that provide instructional information in a graphical form with some textual elements. Using them can imbue the page with some visual interest and often makes the information more easily understood. To enhance comprehension, care should be taken to label the graphic well.

For maps, you have the same choices as with the other types of illustrations above: scanning the work of an illustrator, creating your own map on a computer with a paint or draw program, or using clip art. Clip art is readily available for maps of the globe, continents, regions of the world, individual countries, or states of the United States. For more detailed maps, you may need to

FIGURE 4.3 Landscape for Cartoon

FIGURE 4.4 Protoceratops for Cartoon

FIGURE 4.5 Apatosaurus for Cartoon

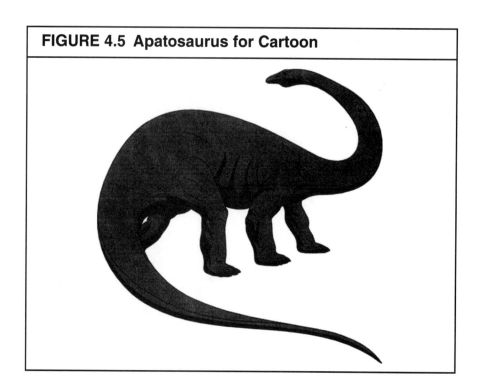

FIGURE 4.6 Archaeopteryx for Cartoon

FIGURE 4.7 Four Graphics Integrated into One Cartoon

We can't be extinct. I haven't seen anything about it on e-mail.

find an illustrator or cartographer, but there may be an electronic source. For example, maps of detailed areas in the United States are available electronically either on CD or on the WWW from the Bureau of the Census's TIGERline mapping files. (http:// www.census.gov/)

Diagrams are usually so specific that it is likely that you will need either to scan in an existing diagram, have an illustrator draw one, or draw it yourself in a paint or draw program if it is simple enough. It should be clean and not cramped. Again, make sure that it is well labeled so that the graphic speaks for itself.

Charts come in a variety of forms and often can be created in a spreadsheet or database program, for example, and imported into your page-layout program. **They should be used sparingly.** Their effective use is dependent on whether the information would be better conveyed in a graphical format or purely with text.

Pie charts are circular and give a visual breakdown of percentages of parts of the whole. They are best used to show broad categories so as not to cut the pie too narrowly.

Bar graphs use vertical bars to compare quantitative items. The number of books checked out by faculty, by students, and by staff could be graphically represented by a bar graph. A bar graph could be drawn easily in a page-layout program, but be sure of your calculations so that it is done to exact scale. And don't forget to label the bars.

A graph is a two-dimensional matrix that shows quantitative data over time so that trends become visible. How many times did that occur six months ago? three months ago? last month? what is the progression? Be careful that both the horizontal and vertical axes are labeled and that the line cutting across the graph is accurately drawn.

Tables also feature a two-dimensional matrix, but do not graph points of convergence. Instead, textual or numeric data fill the table's cells. Most tables have a primary reading direction, either along the vertical or horizontal axis. Make sure that the labeling makes this clear. Lines and tinted screens can improve the clarity of a table to a great extent.

All of these types of informative graphics (shown in Figure 4.8) should be placed in close proximity to the text they are augmenting. They need to be large enough to be clearly read and understood. They must be distinctly labeled, and the text for the labeling may be in a different typeface from the overall text on the page. They should not be overly detailed or complex; an informative graphic that is difficult to understand is not very informative. Highlight only the most important information in your chart, table, or graph.

FIGURE 4.8 Tables, Charts, and Graphs

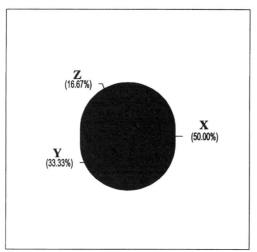

Pie Chart

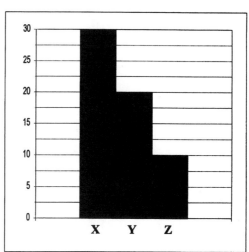

Bar Graph

Diagram

Table

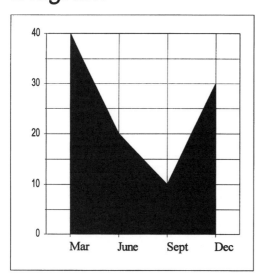

	Allocated	Spent	Free
Sciences	$20,000	$20,000	0
Biology	$8,000	$8,400	-400
Chemistry	$6,000	$5,800	200
Earth	$2,000	$2,700	-700
Math	$2,000	$1,600	400
Physics	$2,000	$1,500	500

DECORATIVE OPTIONS

Lines, boxes, and tinted screens are decorative graphic elements that you can apply as finishing touches to a publication. All three are used to separate text, break up a page, and emphasize certain elements. All should complement the design of a page rather than confound it. Decorative borders and corner designs are other related possibilities.

LINES OR RULES

Lines on a page are called rules in layout terminology. Lines separate text and provide emphasis. They can be drawn to any number of widths (measured in points—see Figure 4.9), but generally should be kept light. Too many or too heavy lines can make a page too dark. Bear in mind that heavier lines don't need to stretch as long to separate two sections of text; you can also run reversed white type through a heavy black line to lighten it up. Remember too that heavier lines need more white space around them. Lines can be drawn either horizontally to separate different sections and stories or vertically to separate columns of text. Lines can even be drawn diagonally for labeling figures.

BOXES

Boxes can be used to frame a photograph or illustration or to separate a section of text as a sidebar or nameplate. With page-layout software, they can be drawn anywhere on a page, to any size, with square or rounded corners, and with a variety of line widths. You can even draw a box around the whole page if you want, although that is not advisable because it tends to make the page look too constricted. Boxes treat text like illustrations and direct the reader's eyes to the text within their boundaries. Boxes should be the same width as a full column or two or more full columns together, with ample margins around the boxed text. Be careful; boxes can be overdone. Their overuse can chop up a page too much and destroy its integrity.

TINTED SCREENS

Tinted screens are gray-tinted boxes (on a black-and-white page— see Figure 4.10). Like regular boxes, they can be drawn to any size, anywhere on a page, with square or rounded corners, with a variety of line widths, or even with no lines at all. Tinted screens also separate text for emphasis and break up a page. The one thing to be careful of is that the weight of your typeface allows

FIGURE 4.9 Typographic Lines or Rules

Lines or Rules

Hairline
_____

.5 point line
_____

1 point line
_____

2 point line
_____

4 point line
_____

6 point line
_____

8 point line
_____

12 point line
_____

Double line
_____

Scotch line
_____

Scotch line
_____

Scotch line
_____

1 point broken line
- - - - - - - - - - - - - -

3 point broken line
▬ ▬ ▬ ▬ ▬ ▬ ▬ ▬ ▬ ▬ ▬ ▬

6 point broken line
■ ■ ■ ■ ■ ■ ■ ■ ■ ■ ■ ■

Reversed line
_____

the text to be clearly deciphered through the tint. Boldface will probably be necessary with text in a tinted box.

FINAL TOUCHES

This chapter has primarily discussed black-and-white graphic elements. Even if you have no color printer and are using no color illustrations or photographs, color still can be part of your publication. A commercial printer can add overlays to the printing process so that certain text or rules or tints are produced in a color other than black. Digital pages, of course, will be awash in color: color photographs, color illustrations, colored text, and colored backgrounds will all serve to brighten your WWW page.

FIGURE 4.10 Tinted Screens

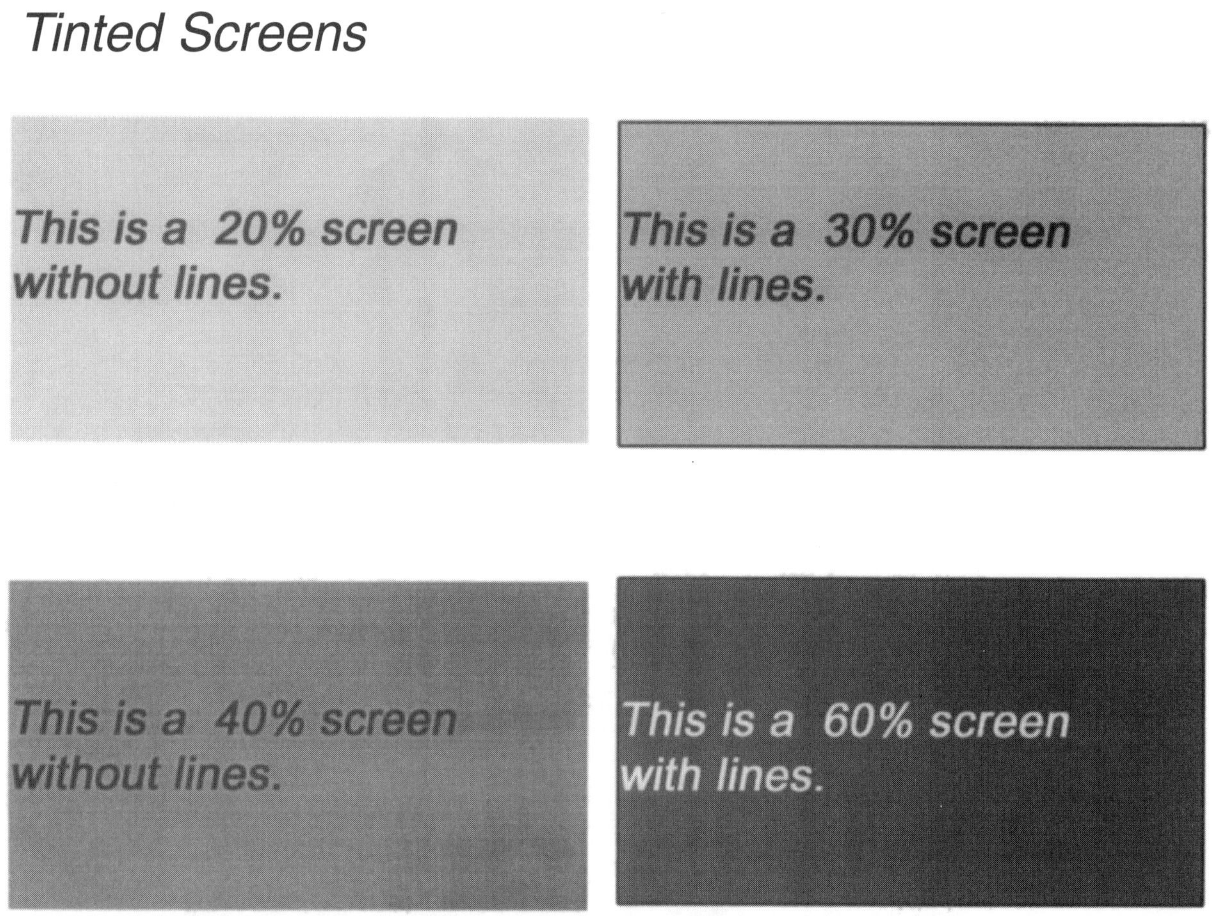

Tinted Screens

This is a 20% screen without lines.

This is a 30% screen with lines.

This is a 40% screen without lines.

This is a 60% screen with lines.

Used judiciously, visual elements provide the final polish to your publication. They make it look sharp, attract attention to the text, and add to the reader's understanding of the information conveyed by the page. They are the most obvious example of the power of desktop publishing. How they and the other building blocks of desktop publishing can be used best for specific types of library publications is described in the following sections.

SECTION 2
NEWSLETTERS

5 SOMETHING TO SAY: PLANNING A NEWSLETTER

Newsletters. You see them every day in your professional and personal lives; you may even read some of them. But what are newsletters? What is it that makes some of them attractive and compelling, while others are instantly deposited into the nearest trash can?

Major Questions to Answer When Planning a Newsletter

- Who is your audience?
- What do you want to say?
- What stories will you have?
- Who will write them?
- What is your budget?
- What is your deadline?
- How many pages will your newsletter have?
- What recurring features and departments will you have?
- Will you use color?
- What will your layout look like?

- What column grid will you use?
- What will be the focal point of each page or spread?
- What typefaces, sizes, and styles will you use?
- How will graphics be incorporated into your layout?
- What stories need graphics?
- What graphics are available?
- How will the newsletter be reproduced and by whom?
- How will the newsletter be distributed and by whom?

At its base, a newsletter is a means of communication. Traditionally, a newsletter was a compilation of timely, pertinent news items produced on a typewriter in a no-frills, no-nonsense, one-column letter format. Often it was printed back-to-back on a single sheet of paper and folded and mailed in a letter envelope.

The advent of desktop publishing changed all of that. Because of desktop publishing's capabilities, newsletters have become one of the most flexible tools for communication by organizations or individuals. And because of that flexibility, they have proliferated to an astounding degree over the last decade. They take a variety of forms today: everything from the aforementioned typewritten letter, to 4–24-page mixes of short articles and eye-catching graphics, to sixty-page journal/newsletter hybrids. What all have in common is their material; newsletters are comprised of expedient, relevant, and generally short articles of interest to a specific audience.

TYPES OF NEWSLETTERS

In a library setting, newsletters are of three main types: the house organ, the public relations vehicle, and the professional connection. While all three are worthy publications, they have vastly different audiences and require vastly different approaches. Each needs to be honest, factually correct, timely, pertinent, and attractive. However, "pertinent" and "attractive" are not absolute values; they depend on the perception of the targeted readers.

HOUSE ORGANS

The term "house organ" carries pejorative connotations of being a publication that primarily conveys propaganda from on high, but an honest house organ is a valuable resource that communicates information to an entire organization **from top to bottom.** The information to be relayed is determined by the organization's management in accordance with their overall goals for the organization.

The house organ will report on the progress of internal projects, potential solutions to problems with computerized systems, promotions and personal news from employees, and upcoming and past meetings. A message from the head of the organization also may be included. The tone of the newsletter is often informal and friendly. One advantage to this type of newsletter is that you can feel really comfortable about who your audience is and what they know. There is a great deal of common knowledge that can be assumed when writing for a house organ, because not only do you know your audience, but they know you as well.

PUBLIC RELATIONS VEHICLES

By contrast, for a public relations vehicle you may not know your audience as well as you would like. In a library setting, a public relations newsletter will be sent to a library's users or potential users. For an academic library that is simple enough; library users are primarily the students, faculty, and staff of the institution. Likewise, in a special library your users generally are the employees of the company or organization. The issue is not so clear-cut for a public library, where your audience is potentially anyone from the local community, and the members' needs, knowledge, and desires are likely to be radically diverse. You might even want to prepare specialized newsletters for specific audiences in this case.

In a public relations vehicle you are trying to sell the capabilities or services of your library to your target audience. You may be trying to get patrons to come in and check out your new books, access your catalog or online indexes from their homes or offices, utilize your government document electronic resources, or make use of some new reference service now available. In short, you are sharing information about information with your audience and hoping to make them understand how they can benefit from your services.

The tone of the newsletter is likely to be more formal, but it can still be friendly and inviting. You are trying to present a good face to your audience. Librarians receive a large number of newsletters of this type from vendors and publishers trying to sell their wares, and you can learn a lot about how to frame your public relations vehicle by studying newsletters you receive in the mail from commercial firms. Which ones do you read? Which get thrown away immediately? Attractive design is important, but so is meaningful content. The content needs to be honest and to the point: "What's in it for me?" the reader wants to know.

PROFESSIONAL CONNECTIONS

The professional connection includes all the newsletters produced by professional associations, large and small, local and national. This type of newsletter is potentially the most interesting and valuable to librarians, but in practice is often very dull indeed.

The first advantage to the professional connection as a publication is that you know your audience. They are professional librarians like you. The organization may represent all cataloguers nationwide, documents librarians of a particular state, all librarians interested in automation issues, just those librarians interested in desktop publishing, or any number of other permutations of your interests and professional standing.

The second advantage is what you have in common with your audience. With the house organ the only thing members of your audience may have in common is that they all work for the same organization. Members of a professional association, however, share at least some common professional interests. What that means for the content of your newsletter is that articles can go into much more depth and be of much greater interest and value to the reader.

The newsletter of a professional association can report on the activities of that organization and its individual members, but it can also feature articles on relevant topics of general interest. In this way, the newsletter can sometimes usurp the role of journals in furthering the understanding of professional interests. Its tone can vary from that of a small local organization, which may have a newsletter with a very informal and even playful personality, to one for a large, national, professional association, which is much more likely to be formal—although it still should strive to be inviting.

DEFINING THE MESSAGE

Once you select your audience and choose an appropriate vehicle, the next step in planning a newsletter is to determine what constitutes news for this group. Should you use the *New York Times*'s guideline of "All the news that's fit to print" or go with the editorial carte blanche of *Rolling Stone*, "All the news that fits"? With any luck you won't be forced to adopt a policy of "Any news I can find."

But what is news to your group? What is pertinent to your readers' interests? What do they want to know? What do they need to know? News items should have some importance to your audience. They should educate, inform, or entertain. They should arouse your readers' interest. Their effect on your readers' lives or careers should be clear. They should not be outdated or no longer relevant. If they concern a significant accomplishment of an audience member, then that's all to the good. Readers will have a natural interest in the doings of one of their own.

The question of what is news to your group should not be a difficult one for you to answer if you are preparing this newsletter for the library for which you work or an association to which you belong. The newsletter's reason for being should mirror that of the parent library or association, that is, to disseminate skillfully good information to those who need it. Within constraints.

WORKING WITH A BUDGET

Just as a library's ability to buy books or provide networked electronic resources is constrained by realities of time and money, so will be your newsletter. What you need to know next to plan your newsletter is your budget. How much money is available? How much can you spend? What happens if you go over budget?

Your budget will affect how often you publish, how many pages in your publication, what kind and size of paper on which you print, how the newsletter will be reproduced, whether you will use color or photographs, and how the newsletter will be distributed. Obviously all of these factors will have an impact on your design and layout for the newsletter, so you need to know just how much you can afford right from the start.

The examples in this book will assume your newsletter has a low-to-moderate budget. By this, I mean that you may have been able to have the organization buy a good page-layout program, but you will not be able to afford to work with color photographs or illustrations. I also assume that you probably will opt for reproducing your master pages via a photocopier rather than a print shop's more costly printing process. And if you choose not to have your master pages professionally printed, then you will not be planning on working with any overly complicated illustrations like photographs—even if you have access to a scanner. Photographs can be photocopied and cut and pasted onto your masters, but each generation of photocopy causes additional degeneration of the quality. Plus, with desktop publishing you are trying to avoid cut-and-paste methods and to enjoy its facilities for manipulation of graphics—resizing, cropping, overlaying with text, and so forth.

In terms of length, you may want to keep to eight pages or less, because if you jump to twelve pages, it's going to take more than one postage stamp to mail the newsletter first class, and that will significantly impact your budget.

As you can see, money is a very big factor in how your newsletter is going to look. The important thing to remember is that even if you are working within the budgetary constraints outlined above, that is no excuse for not turning out an attractive, intelligent publication. If you're not working with color or photographs, that's too bad, but there are scores of illustrations and other graphical elements you can use to accent the design of your page. Likewise, professional printing is wonderful, but as long as your publication is kept clean and simple and features both a nice balance and contrast of black and white, then a professional quality photocopier will return professional results from your master pages.

FIRST IMPRESSIONS

In developing your newsletter, you will discover that all the elements are interconnected—especially to the budget. For example, the first page a reader sees is probably the most important page; it needs to draw the reader in. If you are going to mail your newsletter in a large envelope, then the first page the reader will see is the cover or front page. However, that approach takes more time (stuffing envelopes) and money (postage). Perhaps you will be folding and stapling the newsletter and mailing it by itself. Now the first page the reader sees is the back page with the mailing info. Furthermore, if you are going to fold the newsletter, how will you do it? In half? In thirds? This decision has obvious implications for the layout of that back mailer page in particular.

So let's assume the path of least resistance and fold the publication in half (that's one fewer fold for each of however many copies you will have). In this case, the back page is your most important, and it is largely taken up with mailing information (return address, mailing label, and postage). But there is still roughly half a page of blank space. How can it be spruced up to attract a reader's attention? Many times a newsletter will include the publication's masthead (names and positions of newsletter staff, editorial address and policy, and copyright information) or a final short article on the back page.

The problem with placing the masthead here is that it does nothing to encourage the reader to open the publication. The masthead is necessary, but usually the reader does not care about that information. The problem with placing a short article or the end of a longer article from the interior on the back page is that it often looks out of place there—especially when your back page is not really your back page, i.e., it is not the last page the reader will encounter. The design and layout of the mailer is distinct from the general layout of the newsletter and an article may look funny on that page, as if it didn't fit inside and was not particularly important.

Another approach is to put the table of contents on the mailer. That can be very effective. It fills a good portion of the space and can draw the reader inside. A related approach is to use teasers on the back page. Teasers are catchy phrases that colorfully describe what's inside or perhaps even an overriding theme to the issue if there is one.

Another good use of extra mailer space is the organization's logo or an attractive graphic that fits in with the organization or with accompanying teasers. The key is to give the reader a good reason to open your publication.

Your next task in producing a newsletter is write down what recurring features or departments will be in your newsletter. Your publication will have mailer info, a masthead, and a nameplate. It should have a table of contents, a calendar of upcoming events, and at least one feature article. It also may have an editorial or message from the head of the organization, a letters to the editor section, and a section for very short, two-to-three-line announcements.

Once you know what features will be in each issue, you can think about your layout so that you will know what space is available for news items. When considering your layout, it's best to think with a pencil or keyboard/mouse. In other words, your layout is a graphic design; it needs to be designed graphically. Your mock layout should be rough, quick, and simple. It's intended to let you see how the parts will fit together. The actual work will be in fitting that size 10 foot in the size 9 or size 11 shoe that's available.

The mock layout will take into account all recurring features and will give you a good approximation of how much space is available and where so you know how much material you need. Figures 5.1 and 5.2 offer two distinct approaches taken to the same newsletter with the same recurring features. In both instances, the grid is based on two columns, which is a good layout for the beginner to work with for a newsletter because it is the easiest to make look presentable. If you are not a novice or simply like a graphic design challenge, you may want to try a three-column layout, which is also very good for newsletters. It is more flexible but also more complicated because it increases the design possibilities. Columns can also vary in size, as was discussed in chapter 2.

The pages in Figure 5.1 are designed to be printed back-to-back and corner-stapled, i.e., page one is backed by page two, page three is backed by page four, and so on. This is cheaper and more easily disassembled should the reader want to rip out the program agenda backed with a map of the meeting location. Its disadvantage is that individual $8\frac{1}{2}$" x 11" sheets with a staple in the corner do not look as professional as do saddle-stitched (stapled along the fold of 11" x 17" sheets) publications no matter how clever your design.

The saddle-stitched design (Figure 5.2) moves the agenda and map pages further back so they detract less from the overall design of the newsletter. They are no longer on one sheet back-to-back but instead on facing pages. In addition, the "Info to Go"

FIGURE 5.1 Layout Sheet #1

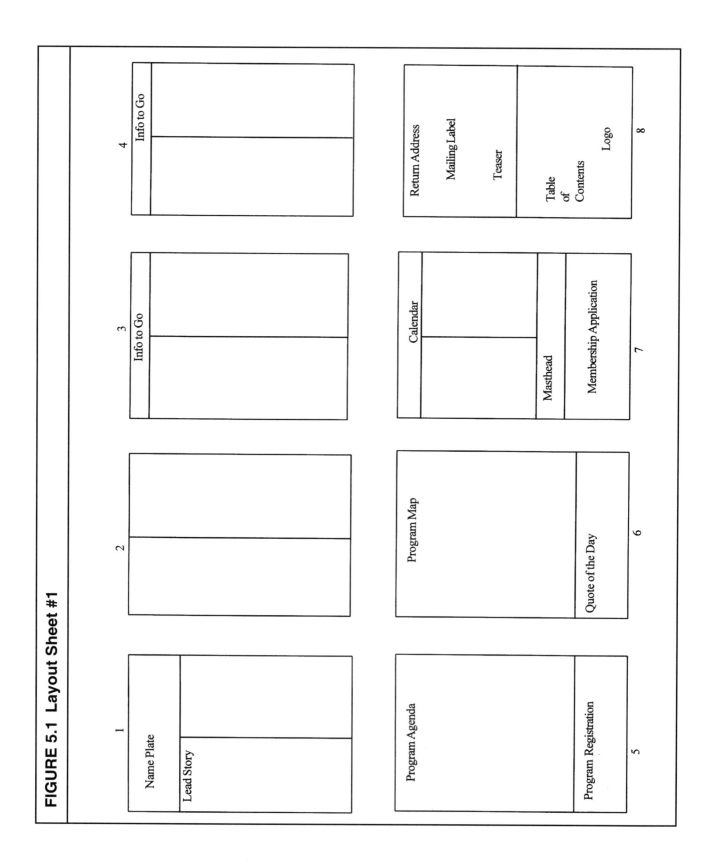

FIGURE 5.2 Layout Sheet #2

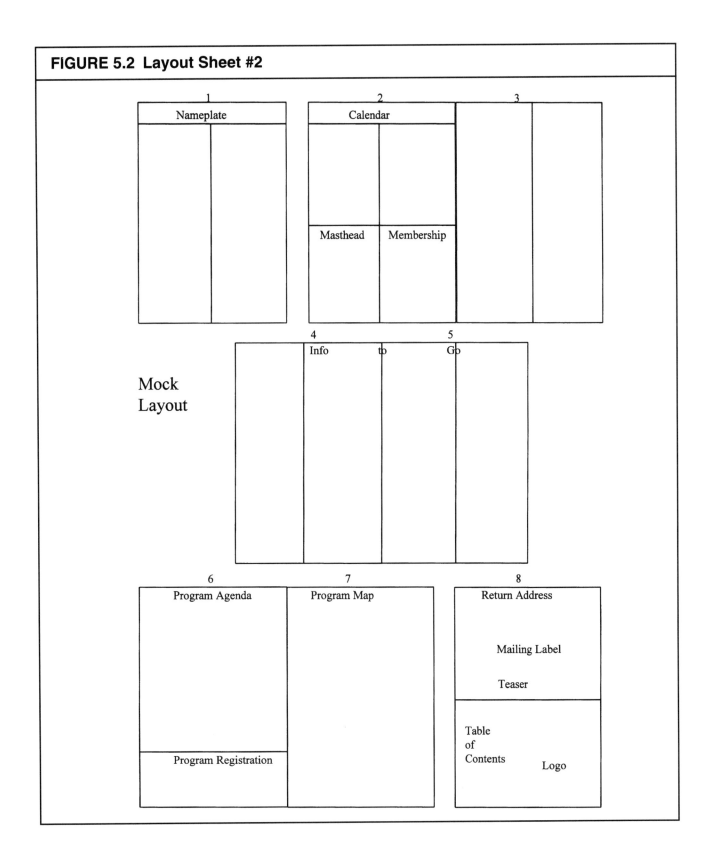

feature article is now on the two facing pages in the middle of the newsletter, making a nice centerpiece. Finally, the features on page seven of the corner-stapled example have been shifted to page two of the saddle-stitched one. To keep this shift from detracting from the overall layout design of the newsletter, the masthead and membership application features have been transformed from a one-column grid to boxed two-column sidebars.

Side-stapling, in which a newsletter is stapled along its left side, is a third option. It permits the use of individual 8 $\frac{1}{2}$" x 11" sheets, copied back-to-back, but stapled so that the layout utilizes facing pages. The point in examining these examples on the rather mundane question of how you will attach the pages of your publication is that everything matters. Every element in the design of a newsletter is part of an interrelated whole that needs to be fully thought out and understood.

WRITING AND EDITING

As you come to an understanding of how you want your newsletter to look and what features it will contain, you will begin to think about what will go into this particular issue. What stories will you cover? Who will write them? When do they need to be completed? The answers to these questions lie in communication. You need to talk to people to find out what is going on that your readers will want to know about. You also need to talk to people to find out who is willing to submit material for the newsletter. Some of this communication will be in person, some by telephone, some by fax, and some by e-mail. Stay in the loop and be aware of what's going on.

When working with writers, be sure to set your due dates far enough in advance so that you have some leeway when they miss the deadline. You'll find that the term "deadline" is a misnomer; it's more like a not-feeling-too-well-line. Writers miss them more than they make them. If you set their deadlines too close to your absolute deadline, you will either be putting out your publication late or scrambling for copy at the last minute. Always have a plan B with extra pieces already written that you can insert in a last-minute emergency.

If you are assigning longer pieces to outside writers, then you may want to give each writer a copy of the style sheet for the newsletter. The style sheet will list the preferred way your publication handles dates, times, numbers, special terminology, spelling, and capitalization. If a writer is only writing a short piece for you, then the style sheet is probably overkill. You can quickly clean up the copy in a shorter piece.

Also, when editing the work of writers, take a good look at each article's lead sentence. The lead should draw you into the piece. Don't be afraid to edit someone else's work. You are the editor, and the publication as a whole is a reflection of you. Make the words as good as they can be.

TYPOGRAPHY AND GRAPHICS

In desktop publishing, style sheet also refers to a feature of page-layout programs that allows you to select what typeface family, styles, and sizes you will be using for different kinds of text. One of the last parts of planning and first parts of producing a newsletter is making these selections. You will want to experiment with "dummy" text to see what typeface looks best for your publication. What you will come up with will look something like this:

Body text: Times Roman, 11 point, leading 13 point, justified, block paragraphs

Headlines: Helvetica, bold, 24 point, leading 28, kerned, ragged right, upper and lower case

Subheads: Helvetica, bold, 18 point, leading 21, kerned, ragged right, upper and lower case

Drop caps: Times Roman, bold, 48 point

Captions: Helvetica, italic, 9 point

Footers: Helvetica, italic, 9 point

It is likely that the typefaces, styles, and sizes you choose will be entirely different from the above choices, but it is important to codify your choices. It will make your life a lot easier as you try to keep the style of your newsletter consistent from page to page and issue to issue. You also need to address many of the other issues discussed in chapters 2 and 3. Will your columns be aligned? Will your text be justified? Are your chosen typefaces readable, legible, and appropriate?

Finally, the last piece to consider in planning your newsletter is how graphic elements will fit into your design. Take an inventory of the text pieces that will be included and fit them into your mock layout. Try to envision how each page will look with just the text, and then decide how you can improve the overall appearance of the pages with visual elements. What items or areas of the page could use an illustration? What illustrations do you have readily available? Are there statistics in the text that could be better expressed by charts or graphs? If you can't come up with an appropriate graphic, are there text-oriented graphics that can brighten the page? Should you use drop or stick-up caps to begin articles? Should there be more white space? Should you consider using pull quotes to break up a longer article? Have you contemplated using lines and boxes to emphasize your text and graphics? Will the graphics you've chosen focus the reader where you want?

This is still the planning stage. Experiment. Try lots of approaches. Just remember: when you move to the production stage, use only what complements your planned design and layout. Don't overdo it.

6 PAGE BY PAGE: PRODUCING A NEWSLETTER

Once you have followed the guidelines in chapter 5, you will have planned what you want to accomplish with your newsletter. You will have an idea of who your audience is, what your message is, and how to best convey that message to that audience.

Major Tasks When Producing a Newsletter

- Set up a template file for your newsletter's recurring features, including the name-plate, masthead, mailer, and any other regular departments.
- Make sure that stories are assigned, written, and edited according to your deadline.
- Lay out your stories on your first page according to your planned design.
- Lay out your stories on your interior pages according to your planned design.
- Choose the best of available graphics for your pages.
- Fit those graphics into your pages.
- Add headlines, subheads, pull quotes, initial caps, and any other effects.
- Add boxes, screens, and rules.
- Print test sheets of your pages.
- Check your test layout for balance, unity, proportion, and focus.

We will assume that your budget is not large, and you will not be working with color illustrations. It is possible, though, that you will have color overlays supplied by your printer to graphic elements like heavy rules and tinted screens. Let's also assume your publication will be either bound with saddle-stitched staples or just folded, and it will be sent through the U.S. mail.

You have decided on what features will be recurring in your newsletter and what pieces will be special in this issue. You have arranged for writers or have undertaken to write the entire issue yourself. You have selected the typefaces and typeface styles and sizes for your text. You also have rounded up a number of illustrations and other visuals that you may use to highlight your text. Finally, you have taken an inventory of your puzzle pieces and drawn up a mock layout of what fits where. You are ready to start.

THE FIRST PAGE

The place to start is the "cover," or first page. Most newsletters do not have true covers like a magazine might have, but the first page does need to be designed as if it were the cover, the first page the reader will see.

THE NAMEPLATE

The first page of a newsletter is dominated by the nameplate, which lists the publication's title. The nameplate may be supplemented by the publication's subtitle if applicable (e.g., "the newsletter of the xyz association") and by a dateline that includes volume and/or issue numbers and publication date of the newsletter. Since the nameplate is not likely to change very frequently and because it is relatively important to the overall design of the newsletter, you want to take pains to make it look good. If you have access to a computer draw program with all its graphic capabilities, you may consider designing your nameplate in that and importing it into your page-layout program. However, an attractive nameplate can very easily be designed in your page-layout program as well.

What is the title of your newsletter? If you are taking over the editing of an existing newsletter, then you might not have any say in this matter. However, new editors are able to change things frequently, so you might be able to rename an existing newsletter. With a new publication, naming the newsletter could very well be your responsibility. If so, think short and sharp. The details can be included in a subtitle. A long newsletter title is harder to work with because if the title has too many words, the typeface needs to be small so the title will fit. However, the typeface for your title should be big and bold. It should grab the reader's eye. For similar reasons, the title should be clever and punchy. The title should give the reader a good idea of what this newsletter entails and what may be found in its pages. In very few words.

If your organization goes by an acronym (XYZ), then your title may be as simple as *XYZ News*. If you can add in some clever word play and ear-pleasing effects like alliteration, that's even better. The newsletter for a group of circulation librarians might be called *The Circular* or one for an organization of catalogers could be *The Catalog Card*. (My apologies if these titles are already in use.) Use your imagination, but at the same time, use some judgement. Your audience may find names like those noted above so cute that it puts them off.

I edit a newsletter called *PARLIENEWS: Newsletter of the Philadelphia Area Reference Librarians' Information Exchange.* Let's use that as an example of some of the possible nameplate designs you could use for your newsletter.

The first example takes a very simple approach. On the first page, you draw a box with a tinted screen across the top of all columns in your grid. Centered in that 40 percent tinted box, you run the name of the newsletter in large, boldface type (48 point, Times New Roman). In small type is the subtitle of the newsletter (18 point, Times New Roman, normal type except for the first letters of each word, which are in boldface type). Below the tinted box is the date line in still smaller type (9 point Times New Roman, normal).

As you can see in Figure 6.1 this is a very conservative look. Some might even say dull, but it might be right for your audience. But there are a number of ways to change this nameplate while keeping its simple design. One way is to enlarge the first and last letters of the newsletter name (to 54 point) and to enclose the subtitle in a box overlapping the original box—all within the opening "P" and the closing "S" (see Figure 6.2).

Another way to change the appearance of this nameplate is to change from boldface type on a tinted background to reversed white type in a box with a black background. In addition, the position of the volume and date have been shifted to above the nameplate (see Figure 6.3).

A large black box may be too dark a look for your publication, but you can still utilize reversed type. The smaller subtitle part of your nameplate can accent the page very nicely if it is set in a black bar with reversed white type. You might find that using rules instead of boxes gives your nameplate a more appealing and open look. For further contrast, you might use sans serif text (Helvetica) for the subtitle while the title remains in serif text. The date line remains above the title so as not to interfere with the nice break given the page by the black subtitle bar (see Figure 6.4).

If your organization has a logo, it could be included in the nameplate to establish instant recognition of the parent organization. In this case, shown in Figure 6.5, the subtitle has been moved alongside the title in order to provide balance to the logo.

As has been discussed at length in earlier chapters, typefaces carry many characteristics that help establish the personality of a page and/or publication. When designing a feature as important as the nameplate, you need to keep that in mind. Times New Roman is familiar, comfortable, and overused. Perhaps you want

FIGURE 6.1 Nameplate

PARLIENEWS

NEWSLETTER OF THE
PHILADELPHIA AREA REFERENCE LIBRARIANS' INFORMATION EXCHANGE

| September 1995 | Number 89 |

FIGURE 6.2 Nameplate with Enlarged First and Last Letters

PARLIENEWS
NEWSLETTER OF THE PHILADELPHIA AREA
REFERENCE LIBRARIANS' INFORMATION EXCHANGE
September 1995
Number 89

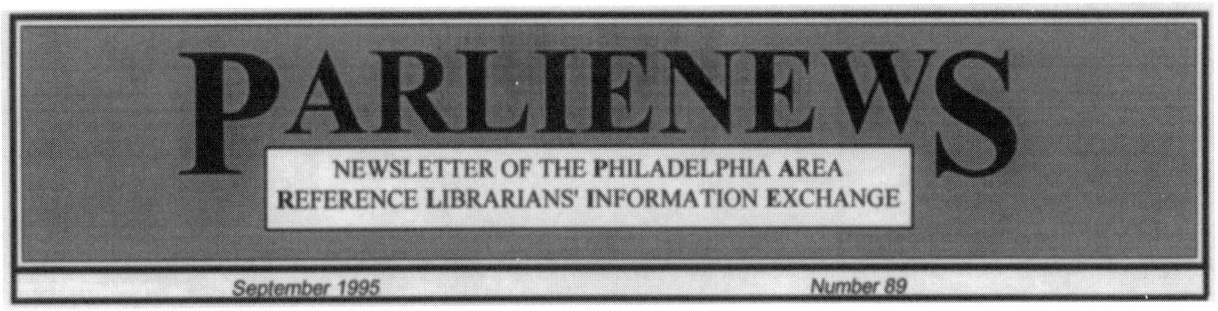

similar type characteristics, but with a less familiar look. There are countless options to choose from. Or you may want your nameplate to convey a completely different mood from the formal look of Times New Roman. Try the cleaner look of a sans serif face like Futura or Univers. Or, as in Figure 6.6, Avant Garde might convey the contemporary, cutting-edge character you want your newsletter to express. Or you may strive to promote an informal look to your publication, as in Figure 6.7. Try a script face like Brush Script.

Finally, there is no rule that says that you must run your nameplate across the top of the page. One advantage to desktop publishing is that you can write text at any angle. One striking way to design your cover is to rotate the text of your title so that it is perpendicular to the orientation of the page and to run your nameplate up the side of the cover (see Figure 6.8). This will narrow the text columns on that first page, but you will gain space at the top of the page. This type of design is very eye-catching although more difficult to read. If you are going to use this approach, make

FIGURE 6.3 Nameplate with Reversed Type

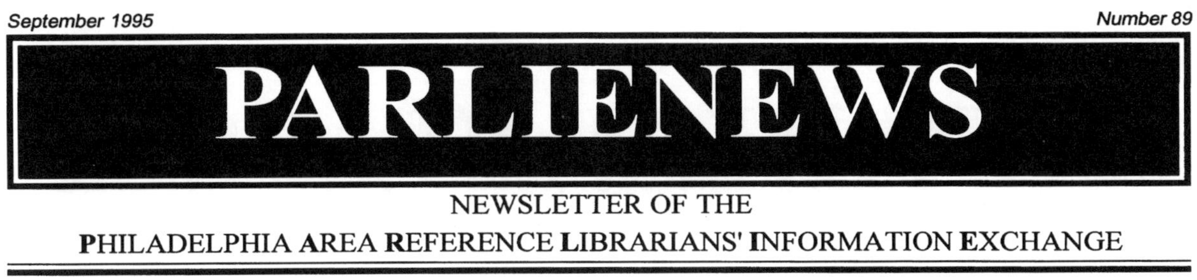

September 1995
Number 89
PARLIENEWS
NEWSLETTER OF THE
PHILADELPHIA AREA REFERENCE LIBRARIANS' INFORMATION EXCHANGE

FIGURE 6.4 Nameplate Without Box

September 1995   *Number 89*

PARLIENEWS

PHILADELPHIA AREA REFERENCE LIBRARIANS' INFORMATION EXCHANGE

sure your title fits the height of the page. You may want to lengthen or shorten the title if you plan to run it along the side of the page.

SETTING UP A TEMPLATE

Once you have constructed your nameplate so that you are pleased with it, it is time to begin setting up the general layout of your publication with all the recurring features that you have planned. This set up can then be stored as a template file by most page-layout programs so that when it's time to create issue number two your nameplate, masthead, mailer, and regular departments will be all ready to go (not to mention your column grid, typographic style sheet, margins, number of pages, and page numbers). When you start issue two, you will open your template file in your page-layout program, save it with its new document name, and be ready to import text and graphics into the layout. Also,

FIGURE 6.5 Nameplate with Logo

NEWSLETTER OF THE

**PHILADELPHIA
AREA
REFERENCE
LIBRARIANS'
INFORMATION
EXCHANGE**   # PARLIENEWS

September 1995   *Number 89*

FIGURE 6.6 Nameplate in Avant Garde Type

PARLIENEWS

NEWSLETTER OF THE
PHILADELPHIA AREA REFERENCE LIBRARIANS' INFORMATION EXCHANGE

September 1995   Number 89

---

your page-layout program will probably come with existing template files for newsletters, brochures, and posters that you can use if you like.

Once you have your column grid, typographic style sheet, and margins set up with actual blank pages created, the next step in creating the template is to make master pages. Master pages are a feature of most page-layout software and include a master left page and a master right page. With master pages, you can specify items you want to appear on every page or on every right or left page. In the mock layout described in chapter 5, the column grid was primarily a two-column one, but included a one-column program agenda, a one-column program map page and a one-column mailer on the back page. Because of this mix of one- and two-column pages, columns are not necessarily set up on the master pages of the publication.

You probably want to include a folio on master pages. A folio includes such information as page numbers, publication name, and date or issue numbers (see Figure 6.9). The folio is generally

---

FIGURE 6.7 Nameplate in Brush Script Type

PARLIENEWS

NEWSLETTER OF THE
PHILADELPHIA AREA REFERENCE LIBRARIANS' INFORMATION EXCHANGE

September 1995   Number 89

FIGURE 6.8 Perpendicular Nameplate

September 1995   Number 89
THE NEWSLETTER OF THE
Philadelphia Area Reference Librarians' Information Exchange

FIGURE 6.9 Folio as Footer

run as a footer at the bottom of every page or as a header at the top of every page and can be set up either way on your master pages. Keep in mind that folios are not usually run on front or back pages, so you will have to mask the folio from appearing on those pages. How to do that will vary according to your page-layout program.

Next on your template you want to set up other items common to most issues. Earlier, the importance of the back page was discussed, particularly when the issue is to be folded and mailed, and the back page is the first page the reader will see.

THE MAILER

For a mailer, you will divide the page into sections according to where it will be folded. Assuming you will fold it in half, then one half, usually the bottom, will contain mailing information, and the other half, usually the top, will have some elements to draw the reader into the publication. The table of contents, a teaser line, and an organizational logo were three possible "draws" discussed in chapter 5. The parts of the mailer are the return address, a spot for the mailing label, and a spot for the postage.

So your template back page will be largely empty. Unless you are using bulk mail, all that will appear on the mailer section is the text of the return address, because the label and postage will be applied after the newsletter is printed. As for the other half of the page, the table of contents and teaser line will vary from issue to issue, so they can be left blank on the template. Another approach is to leave a sample table of contents and teaser there as placeholders so that all you have to do is replace some text for each new issue. If you are using a logo, obviously it will not change from issue to issue and should be on the template (see Figure 6.10).

THE MASTHEAD

The masthead is another largely static feature that all newsletters will contain, usually on the inside pages (see Figure 6.11). The masthead gives the attribution information for the publication: the name of the editor and any other staff, the address, telephone number, fax number, and e-mail address for the publication, the frequency of the publication, whether the publication is indexed and if so where, the ISSN, copyright information, subscription rates, and submission details and dates. It is short, essential bibliographic sort of data, but not riveting reading. It is a section almost always skipped by most readers. For these reasons, a typeface in a small point size is appropriate.

FIGURE 6.10 Mailer

DOC SOUP

PARLIENEWS
c/o John Maxymuk
Paul Robeson Library
Rutgers University
Camden, NJ 08101

FIRST CLASS

PHILADELPHIA AREA REFERENCE LIBRARIANS' INFORMATION EXCHANGE

FIGURE 6.11 Masthead

PARLIENEWS, the newsletter of the Philadelphia Area Reference Librarians' Information Exchange, is published preceding every PARLIE meeting. A subscription to the PARLIENEWS is included with membership in PARLIE.

All submissions, questions or suggestions should be addressed to the newsletter editor: **John Maxymuk,** Robeson Library, Rutgers University, Camden, NJ 08101. (609)225-6034. FAX: (609) 225-6428.
INTERNET: MAXYMUK@ZODIAC.RUTGERS.EDU.

To become a member, renew your membership or update your address information, contact the Treasurer **Mxxxxxx Sxxxx,** Falvey Library, Villanova University, Villanova, PA 19085. (999) 999-9999.
INTERNET: SXXXX@XXXX.XXXX.EDU.

OTHER RECURRING FEATURES

Your newsletter may have any number of additional features that will appear in most or all issues. You may regularly run a meeting registration form, or letters to the editor, or calendar information, or some special topics feature in your newsletter. Some of these are unchanging, while others have consistent aspects.

For instance, a calendar listing of upcoming events obviously changes with each issue, but the layout of that page may be unique, and those repeating textual and graphical layout elements can be saved on your template (see Figure 6.12). The calendar may have an unchanging headline set in a special typeface accented by an unchanging graphic design. With all of that saved on your template, the only thing you have to add each issue is the listings themselves.

Your template contains all the aspects of your layout that stay the same from issue to issue. These are the elements that give your publication a unified, consistent appearance. They make up at least half the struggle in designing that first issue, but from the second or third issue on you won't be overly concerned with them any longer if you have taken the time and effort to get them right—right for your publication, at least. On occasion, if you continue to edit this publication long enough, you will want to revisit these template features and give your aging beauty a facelift, but for now it is time to move on to issue-specific layout and design and return to the first page.

FIGURE 6.12 Calendar Listing

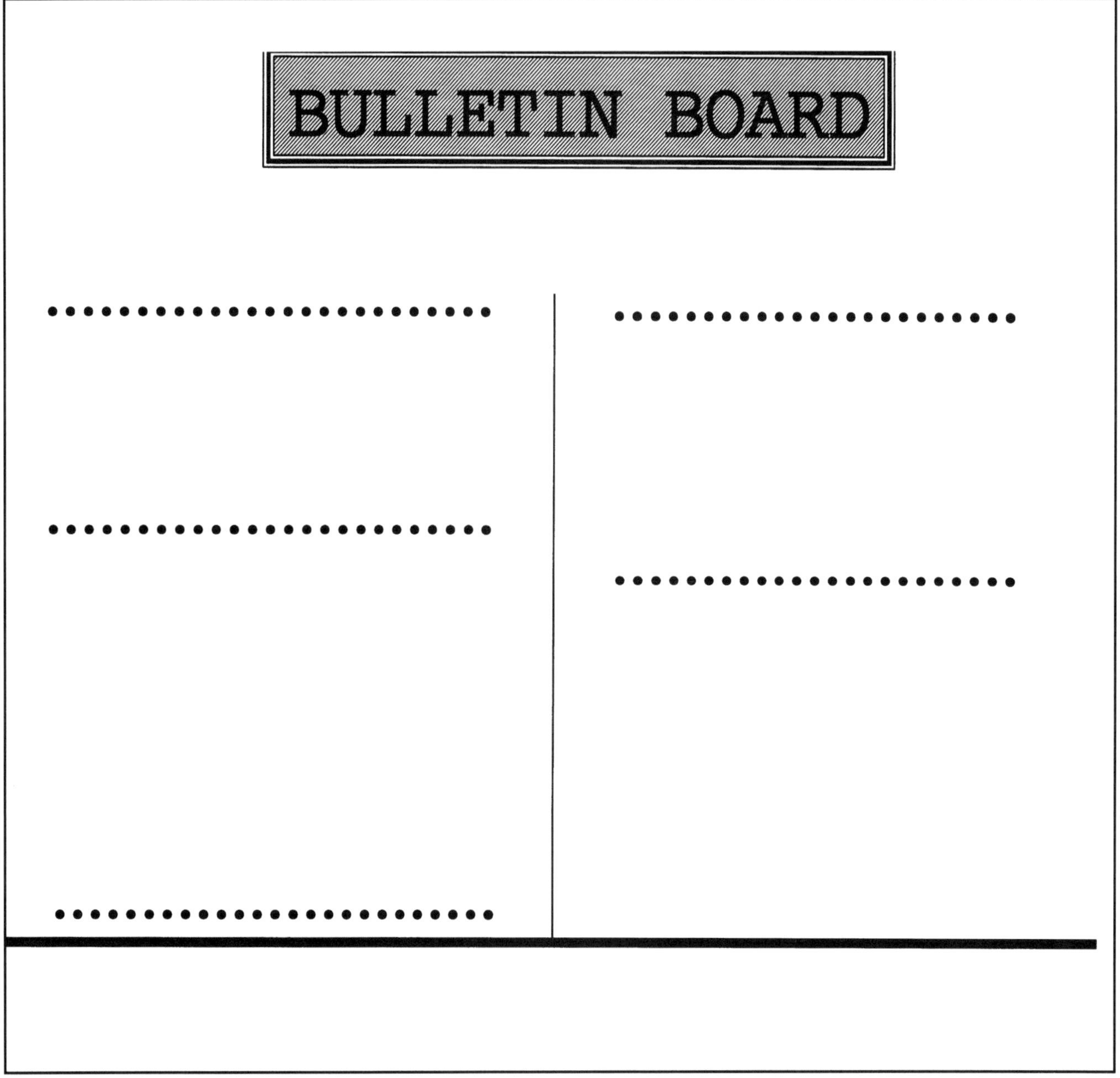

CHOOSING YOUR MAIN STORY

The first question regarding the first page for any particular issue is: What is your main story going to be? The answer to that question depends on a number of factors, the first of which are: Who is your audience, and what are you trying to communicate to them?

If your audience is your fellow workers at the library where you work and your newsletter is a house organ, then your main story may be a message from the library director; or it could be the announcement of a new in-house computer system; or it could concern a new service the library is offering. In the case of a new library service, the story's focus might be how this will improve the standing of the library and what impact this new service will have on library staff. Your main story will usually be a positive one, but if a negative issue needs to be discussed, it can be done here—with a positive spin, of course.

If your audience is primarily patrons and potential patrons and your newsletter is a public relations vehicle, then your lead story almost always will be a positive one focusing on what the library can do for the reader, or new services or materials the library offers. You are trying to engage the reader; you don't want the first story a reader sees in your newsletter to be one describing how records of patrons with overdue books are now being turned over to a collection agency and how legal action will be sought against especially notable miscreants.

Finally, if your audience is made up of fellow librarians and the newsletter is a professional connection, then the topic of your main story is wide open. The most common one would be either coverage of the last meeting or conference held by the association (as in Figure 6.13) or an announcement of the next association meeting with an overview of its topic. However, in this type of newsletter there are scores of options. A member of the association, or the association itself, may have received a special honor. The association may be announcing a new scholarship program or training project. A controversial issue for the profession or a particular segment of it may be discussed. A new type of service or technology or a new application of a current one might be explained. The only thing to consider is whether the story you choose is the one of most interest or significance to your readers.

No matter who your audience is, what type of newsletter it is, or what your message may be, certain things must be considered in order that your main story gets the reader's full attention. The

FIGURE 6.13 Importing Your Main Story

September 1995   Number 89

Government Documentary

Villanova University was once again the site, and government documents was the topic when PARLIE convened last on May 18th 1995. At a meeting entitled "Government Documents Online and Off" five speakers educated a mixed crowd of PARLIE and Delaware Valley Government Documents Group (DVGDG) members on a variety of government information resources.

Our first speaker was Kxx Mxxxxxxxx from Villanova University's Law School. Kxx is primarily responsible for the creation and maintenance of the Villanova Center for Information Law and Policy's home page on the World Wide Web (WWW) (URL=http://www.law.vill.edu), a page widely regarded as one of the best sites on the WWW to locate government information.

In his talk, Kxx ran through the different aspects to the Villanova Web site, giving particular emphasis to its Federal Web Locator which attempts to be a comprehensive organized listing of federal Web sites. In addition, Kxx covered the Federal Court Locator at his site. This page includes links not only to the Supreme Court opinions, but to the Courts of Appeal from the third, fourth, fifth, sixth, ninth and eleventh circuits.

Bxxxx Lxxxxx from the Patent Collection at the Free Library of Philadelphia spoke next. The original patent depository for the area was the Franklin Institute, but in the early 1980s they gave that designation up and transferred their patent records to the Free Library. Bxxx's talk was enlivened with examples and anecdotes. Did you know that Thomas Jefferson was the nation's first patent examiner? Or that to find the patent records for an ice cream sandwich, you'd have to look under "Frozen Edible Confection Between Two Edible Boards?"

The last speaker of the morning was Jxxx Dxxxxxx, now of the Moore School of Art and Design. Jxxx discussed government resources on AIDS available on the Internet.

headline for your main story, like all your headlines, should be big, bold, brief, and catchy. It should connote the content of the story and attract the reader's interest. If your main story is lengthy, extending into interior pages, you may want to break up your text with subheads and pull quotes. These two features can serve the additional function of creating interest in the content of an article if they are catchy and intriguing.

Another area to focus on in your main story is its lead, the opening sentence or two of the piece. Is it well written? Does it draw the reader in and make him or her want to read more and learn more? The story's lead can also be graphically highlighted by using oversized initial letters—either a stick-up cap or a drop cap—to emphasize where the reader should begin (see Figure 6.14).

ADDING GRAPHIC ELEMENTS

All of the design elements need to work well on each page. However, there is a special emphasis placed on the design of the first page because it is the first impression your reader gets of your publication, and first impressions can be lasting ones. Make sure everything is right on that first page. Add the other stories you plan to run there, and keep text, graphics, and white space in balance, but not so symmetrical that the effect is monotonous (see Figure 6.15). Take care to avoid the "tombstone" look—a page with perfectly aligned side-by-side heads and stories.

Place any illustrations or other visuals you have planned for the page. Do they add to the overall design of the page or detract? Do they accent the content of the text or is the connection between the text and accompanying graphic enigmatic and confusing? Is there a better use for this space?

Finally, if you have a sidebar (a shorter piece related to the main story), now is the time to create the box or tinted screen around it. If you are going to display vertical and/or horizontal rules on the page, now is the time to draw them (see Figure 6.16). Hairline vertical rules between columns can add a very attractive finish to your page, although some prefer not to use them. Horizontal rules can provide a page with clear delineations. But as with every other design element, there are no absolutes. Important factors to weigh include: are the lines too heavy for the balance and contrast of the page? Do the lines and boxes overpower the page and give it a "boxy" feel? Intuition and experience are your best aids here.

FIGURE 6.14 Adding an Initial Drop Cap

September 1995   Number 89

Government Documentary

Villanova University was once again the site, and government documents was the topic when PARLIE convened last on May 18th 1995. At a meeting entitled "Government Documents Online and Off" five speakers educated a mixed crowd of PARLIE and Delaware Valley Government Documents Group (DVGDG) members on a variety of government information resources.

Our first speaker was Kxx Mxxxxxxx from Villanova University's Law School. Ken is primarily responsible for the creation and maintenance of the Villanova Center for Information Law and Policy's home page on the World Wide Web (WWW) (URL=http://www.law.vill.edu), a page widely regarded as one of the best sites on the WWW to locate government information.

In his talk, Kxx ran through the different aspects to the Villanova Web site, giving particular emphasis to its Federal Web Locator which attempts to be a comprehensive organized listing of federal Web sites. In addition, Kxx covered the Federal Court Locator at his site. This page includes links not only to the Supreme Court opinions, but to the Courts of Appeal from the third, fourth, fifth, sixth, ninth and eleventh circuits.

Bxxxx Lxxxxx from the Patent Collection at the Free Library of Philadelphia spoke next. The original patent depository for the area was the Franklin Institute, but in the early 1980s they gave that designation up and transferred their patent records to the Free Library. Bxxx's talk was enlivened with examples and anecdotes. Did you know that Thomas Jefferson was the nation's first patent examiner? Or that to find the patent records for an ice cream sandwich, you'd have to look under "Frozen Edible Confection Between Two Edible Boards?"

The last speaker of the morning was Jxxx Dxxxxxx, now of the Moore School of Art and Design. Jxxx discussed

You will follow the same procedure in laying out your planned design for interior pages as you did for the first page. Decide on the placement of your stories. Import them. Add graphic elements and illustrations. Add finishing touches. Keep it simple, but make it look snazzy.

INTERIOR PAGE DESIGN

The most important thing to keep in mind when filling your interior pages is that you are laying out two facing pages at once. You have taken that into account with your design and now must put that into practice with your layout—particularly as you add the graphic elements to finish off your pages. Make sure you stop periodically and look at both pages simultaneously on the screen. With this view, you won't be able to read the words on the page because they will be too small, but you will be able to see how your overall layout looks. Occasionally, print out the pages as you are working on them to see how they really look.

Does the appearance compare favorably to your original design? Is there too much text and not enough white space? Are there too many illustrations or other graphics? Is the page overwhelmed by one element or is there balance among all the elements with emphasis given to that feature you want emphasized?

The middle two pages in particular are often emphasized in newsletters; they constitute the centerpiece of your publication. As with a holiday table, the centerpiece of your newsletter can brighten the whole publication by giving it some real pizzazz. If you are using a professional printer, graphics and other elements can overlap the gutter between the two pages. (Laser printers cannot extend or "bleed" to the edge of the page; they always leave about a quarter of an inch margin on the printed page no matter how it looks on your screen.)

Even without "bleeds," your centerpiece is a place to put special design ideas, large ones that take two pages into account. It is best to focus the text of your centerpiece onto one topic to really set those two pages apart. You may use multiple articles, but they should all relate to a single subject. This is a good spot to examine an issue from a variety of perspectives or in one in-depth piece. The centerpiece is also a good place to use your graphic elements with flair. Remember, this is desktop publishing so almost anything is possible. If you can conceive something, you can digitize it and bring it into your pages.

FIGURE 6.15 Adding Other Stories and an Illustration

PARLIENEWS
NEWSLETTER OF THE
PHILADELPHIA AREA REFERENCE LIBRARIANS' INFORMATION EXCHANGE

September 1995   Number 89

Government Documentary

Villanova University was once again the site, and government documents was the topic when PARLIE convened last on May 18th 1995. At a meeting entitled "Government Documents Online and Off" five speakers educated a mixed crowd of PARLIE and Delaware Valley Government Documents Group (DVGDG) members on a variety of government information resources.

Our first speaker was Kxx Mxxxxxxx from Villanova University's Law School. Kxx is primarily responsible for the creation and maintenance of the Villanova Center for Information Law and Policy's home page on the World Wide Web (WWW) (URL=http://www.law.vill.edu), a page widely regarded as one of the best sites on the WWW to locate government information.

In his talk, Kxx ran through the different aspects to the Villanova Web site, giving particular emphasis to its Federal Web Locator which attempts to be a comprehensive organized listing of federal Web sites. In addition, Kxx covered the Federal Court Locator at his site. This page includes links not only to the Supreme Court opinions, but to the Courts of Appeal from the third, fourth, fifth, sixth, ninth and eleventh circuits.

Bxxxx Lxxxxx from the Patent Collection at the Free Library of Philadelphia spoke next. The original patent depository for the area was the Franklin Institute, but in the early 1980s they gave that designation up and transferred their patent records to the Free Library. Bxxx's talk was enlivened with examples and anecdotes. Did you know that Thomas Jefferson was the nation's first patent examiner? Or that to find the patent records for an ice cream sandwich, you'd have to look under "Frozen Edible Confection Between Two Edible Boards?"

The last speaker of the morning was Jxxx Dxxxxxx, now of the Moore School of Art and Design. Jxxx discussed

"Your Honor, I Really Meant to Send in My Dues"

Included in this issue of the newsletter is a membership renewal form (page 7). If you have not renewed your membership for 1996, complete the form and mail it to the treasurer as soon as possible. You will NOT receive a renewal reminder in the mail. Membership must be current in order to receive future issues of the Newsletter. Send in your dues now or tell it to the Judge.

Our Next Attraction

PARLIE's second fall meeeting will take place in the Lecture Room at Temple University's Paley Library on Tuesday, December 6th from 9AM to Noon. The topic is CD-ROM technology today and its implications for libraries. Speakers will address how to make your own compact disc product, the state of "writeable" technology and the potential archival uses of CD-ROM. Paley is located on 13th Street and Norris Streets.

Blue Rocks Jocks Shocked

Unfortunately, turnout to the PARLIE-sponsored Wilmington Blue Rocks baseball game on August 10th was slight. Seats were cheap and very good. The weather was great, and the baseball was sharp and fun. The Hillcats won. It's too bad that most of you missed it. Try a Blue Rocks game next year. Or try the Trenton Thunder or the Reading Phillies.

FIGURE 6.16 Finishing the Page with Rules

September 1995   Number 89

Government Documentary

Villanova University was once again the site, and government documents was the topic when PARLIE convened last on May 18th 1995. At a meeting entitled "Government Documents Online and Off" five speakers educated a mixed crowd of PARLIE and Delaware Valley Government Documents Group (DVGDG) members on a variety of government information resources.

Our first speaker was Kxx Mxxxxxx from Villanova University's Law School. Kxx is primarily responsible for the creation and maintenance of the Villanova Center for Information Law and Policy's home page on the World Wide Web (WWW) (URL=http://www.law.vill.edu), a page widely regarded as one of the best sites on the WWW to locate government information.

In his talk, Kxx ran through the different aspects to the Villanova Web site, giving particular emphasis to its Federal Web Locator which attempts to be a comprehensive organized listing of federal Web sites. In addition, Kxx covered the Federal Court Locator at his site. This page includes links not only to the Supreme Court opinions, but to the Courts of Appeal from the third, fourth, fifth, sixth, ninth and eleventh circuits.

Bxxxx Lxxxxx from the Patent Collection at the Free Library of Philadelphia spoke next. The original patent depository for the area was the Franklin Institute, but in the early 1980s they gave that designation up and transferred their patent records to the Free Library. Bxxx's talk was enlivened with examples and anecdotes. Did you know that Thomas Jefferson was the nation's first patent examiner? Or that to find the patent records for an ice cream sandwich, you'd have to look under "Frozen Edible Confection Between Two Edible Boards?"

The last speaker of the morning was Jxxx Dxxxxxx, now of the Moore School of Art and Design. Jxxx discussed
Continued on page 2

"Your Honor, I Really Meant to Send in My Dues"

Included in this issue of the newsletter is a membership renewal form (page 7). If you have not renewed your membership for 1996, complete the form and mail it to the treasurer as soon as possible. You will NOT receive a renewal reminder in the mail. Membership must be current in order to receive future issues of the Newsletter. Send in your dues now or tell it to the Judge.

Our Next Attraction

PARLIE's second fall meeeting will take place in the Lecture Room at Temple University's Paley Library on Tuesday, December 6th from 9AM to Noon. The topic is CD-ROM technology today and its implications for libraries. Speakers will address how to make your own compact disc product, the state of "writeable" technology and the potential archival uses of CD-ROM. Paley is located on 13th Street and Norris Streets.

Blue Rocks Jocks Shocked

Unfortunately, turnout to the PARLIE-sponsored Wilmington Blue Rocks baseball game on August 10th was slight. Seats were cheap and very good. The weather was great, and the baseball was sharp and fun. The Hillcats won. It's too bad that most of you missed it. Try a Blue Rocks game next year. Or try the Trenton Thunder or the Reading Phillies.

Once you have followed the above procedure and laid out all the pages of your publication in your page-layout program, the next step is publishing your newsletter, the subject of chapter 7.

7 PUTTING IT ON PAPER: PUBLISHING A NEWSLETTER

Well, you laid out the pages in your page-layout program without any problems, right?! That is usually not the case. Many problems can and will arise, but the two most common ones in layout relate to the most important part of your newsletter, the text. The words communicate your message, and that is the point of publishing the newsletter, but the words may not fit. You may have too much copy or not enough for any particular page.

Major Tasks When Publishing a Newsletter

- Print final test sheets of your pages.
- Proof text, graphics, and overall design of the pages.
- Copyedit text, charts, and tables.
- Make final corrections to your pages.
- Print master sheets of your pages.
- Make sure that master sheets are clean copies.
- Deliver master sheets to printer with reproducing specifications.
- If you will be distributing your newsletter by mail, arrange for postage.
- Pick up copies from printer and distribute by mail or any other method previously decided upon.
- Solicit feedback on how your newsletter could be improved.

COPYFITTING PROBLEMS

If you have too much copy, can you shift the excess to another page? If your other pages are filled also, the answer is more intensive editing. Does the article go off on entertaining but unrelated tangents? Then whole sentences can be lopped off. Are parts of the text repetitive? Have you closely looked at every word and phrase for wordiness? An inflated phrase like "at that point in time" can be changed to "then." An extended passive construction like "a meeting was held for the club" is better said as "the club met." Long, flowery terms like "domicile," "discontinuation," or "aperture" are better replaced by "house," "end," and "hole." Active construction is better for most writing, and concise writing is always better for newsletters.

Once you have edited your text to the bone, there are other ways to gain space if your text is still too long. A graphic accompanying the story can be reduced in size or relocated on the page. Other stories on the page perhaps can be combined into a single story with fewer space-consuming headlines. If your story contains any sections of different text like a list of Internet addresses or reference resources or extended quotes, you may be able to slightly reduce the point size of that section (from 11 point to 10 point, for example) without disrupting the overall appearance of the page. Some less-timely stories can be deleted and saved for a future issue. Dealing with too much copy necessitates creativity.

But then, so does having too little copy. It's a good idea to keep a file of space-filler items, i.e., items that are very brief, are of general interest, may be amusing, and have no "expiration date." When you have a big hole in your page, one solution is to plug in one of these fillers. Another approach is to add another graphic as long as the extra graphic "fits" and doesn't throw the whole page out of balance. Or you can add some white space around your headlines, pull quotes, or between articles. You can add subheads as well or distinctive lines and borders.

PROOFING THE NEWSLETTER

Once everything fits, you will print out the pages of your newsletter for what you hope is the last time. It never is, though, because now it is time to proofread your originals. No matter how you plan on printing the newsletter, the copy and graphics need to be clean and free of errors before you publish. Otherwise, you'll have to take up space in your next issue with an embarrassing item with a headline like "Oops, We Goofed." As noted earlier, don't rely solely on your software's spell checkers because they won't catch all errors.

Proofing the newsletter refers primarily to the text, but you are checking the graphics as well. If you wrote most or all of the text in the newsletter, it is a good idea to have someone else proof it. After working with text for an extended period of time, you tend to become overly familiar with it. When you read it, you are no longer seeing every word; you don't have to because you already know what it says. There are tricks you can try, like reading each story backwards or every line from right to left. These will make you look at each word, but will not allow you to comprehend what you are reading. You may catch every misspelling, but incorrect word choices or improper usage can sneak by undetected. Such mistakes will be quickly detected by your readers, and they will be delighted to share them with you.

Even if you are using outside contributors, you will have been working closely with their text while editing it. In which case, you are confronted with the same problem as above: you have become overly familiar with it and will miss things such as inevitable typographic errors that occur in the process of editing text. So, have someone else look at the text to proof it. Reasonably literate colleagues, friends, and spouses are often good candidates to catch your glaring mistakes. Of course, if you overwhelm them with many pages and a deadline of yesterday, they might become ex-colleagues, friends, or spouses. Plan ahead. Allow enough production time to let someone look over your text.

The copyeditor will check the text for misspellings, missing or incorrect punctuation, missing words, inappropriate vocabulary choices, and factual errors. The copyeditor will also check for errors of syntax, or word order, and grammatical, or usage, problems. These kinds of problems might be evident in a lack of agreement between your subject and verb, an inconsistent use of verb tense, the use of misplaced or dangling modifiers, or any other breaches of the commonly understood rules of grammar. When writing, editing, or copyediting, keep either paper or electronic versions of some basic reference books close by: a dictionary, a thesaurus, and books on grammar and writing style.

Beyond copyediting, there are a host of items to check for when proofing the pages for a final time. They can be arranged as checklists within the building blocks of page layout described in the first section of this book. Many, if not most, of these items are best settled in the planning stage. However, the beauty and challenge of desktop publishing is that it is such a fluid process that almost anything can be changed up to the printing of the final masters. The items on these proofing checklists have been discussed in previous chapters, but now is the time for the final check on the total package of your newsletter.

Take a look at Figure 7.1, and see if you can figure out which design principles it violates.

The main problem with Figure 7.1 is that there are too many words on the page. Most readers will be somewhat repelled by

FIGURE 7.1 Bad Design Example #1

COUNCIL REPORT

RESTRUCTURING OF DEPOSITORY LIBRARY PROGRAM:
FALL DEPOSITORY LIBRARY COUNCIL MEETING

The Fall 1992 Depository Library Council meeting was held Oct 19-20, 1992 in Room LM-407 of the Library of Congress Madison Building. Monday morning was an informal preparatory session for Council, and there were updates from Superintendent of Documents Wayne Kelley and Judy Russell, Director, Library Programs Service.

Mr. Kelley talked about the various staff changes that have taken place in LPS and Sales. He has asked a dozen mid-level managers to take on new assignments and asked them to take a fresh and inquisitive eye to their areas of new responsibilities to look for ways to improve their performance. The ultimate goal is to implement change to improve GPO's performance and to create an organization that will serve the needs of the American public in the coming years. Judy Russell then reviewed the various staff changes within LPS and what is to be expected as a result of these changes. A comment was made that the community is concerned about these changes. Mr. Kelley said that if these changes resulted in operational problems to please let him know.

Judy also gave an update on the tactical plans for implementing GPO 2001. Tentative drafts are due to the Public Printer by October 30, 1992. The two plans that fall under Mr. Kelley's supervision are: looking at new electronic and print on demand products and services to satisfy customer agency needs and public desires, and development and implementation of electronic capabilities to serve depository libraries. Judy outlined the key points going into their tactical plans (it will probably be one combined plan), and shared some of the critical events they see happening as a result of the plan.

Lastly, Judy gave an update on GPO's budget situation. GPO did a needs-based budget this year, rather than figuring out how to make do with what is appropriated. They came up with $32.5 million requirement and an appropriation of $29 million. It is assumed that since printing and binding is the largest portion of GPO's costs that substantive cuts will have to go there. GPO is looking at a number of alternatives for dealing

study on the feasibility of disseminating information in electronic formats. In doing so, they are to utilize the assistance of the Community College Distant Learning Center in Owensboro, KY. Despite the fact that the WINDO/Gateway bill didn't pass, GPO is moving ahead in an electronic direction. It is not clear that the program structure established 30 years ago is the best possible way to accommodate electronic technology. Which is why Council is looking at restructuring. The purpose of the questions discussed is to transform the DLP into an institution that continues to meet its mission in an era of drastically changing technology, limited funding, and increased public need.

Question #1 dealt with whether there should be a DLP in the electronic age. How could the program be restructured to fit the realities of the current budget?

Council never came right out and answered this question. Instead it was assumed that there should be a program and Council outlined the goals of such a program. Council later outlined the assumptions it had concerning a restructured program. Assumptions included such things as: information world will be a combination of electronic and print for the foreseeable future; there will be a need for information professionals; technology will be there to support the program; user expectations will change and increase; points of delivery will become more diverse; we'll need to further leverage our resources through cooperative ventures; connectivity to INTERNET/NREN will be available to all libraries; federal/state/local investments in new development will be made over next 5-10 years; information policy environment is uncertain, conflicting and will probably continue; telecommunications issues will also remain uncertain and will be resolved on a much larger scale; there is a need to restructure the DLP; some depository libraries will be partners in change, some will not; and DLP has value.

Question #2 dealt with the goals and objective of the DLP. Are these goals consistent with the member institutions? Are the depository libraries also meeting their responsibility to serve the public?

In looking at the 3 major goals of the program as

Proofing Checklist for Overall Design

- Is there an overall balance among all of the elements that make up each page? Is the page structure well defined?
- Have you used white space well? Does the white space on the page accent and emphasize the text and graphics?
- Is there too much text crammed onto the page so the page is uninviting to read? Or have you laid out just enough text among graphics and white space?
- Do unifying elements like the folio and the column grid help tie together the appearance of the pages of the publication? Have you used a template with your page-layout program to set up recurring unifying elements?
- If there is color, is it used with subtlety, or does it dominate the page?
- Are text and graphics of varying sizes fully integrated into the overall layout of each page?
- Are text items and visual elements related? Do they reinforce each other as well as the overall page?
- If the page is asymmetrically designed, is it still pleasing to the eye? Is the focal point of the page appropriate?
- If the page is symmetrical, is it too symmetrical? Is it centered to the point of monotony with "tombstoned" headlines and mirrored graphic elements?

---

this much unbroken text. The reader's eyes look for the comforting relief of white space. Visuals used smartly and sparsely can attract a reader's attention. Lines and borders can further enhance the page until it becomes a pleasure to behold, as in Figure 7.2.

Now, how about the layout in Figure 7.3? Symmetry to a deadly extreme—it even comes with the aforementioned tombstones. And what does that illustration have to do with anything on the page? The same text is laid out better in Figure 7.4.

Figure 7.5 features some badly used typographic elements. Can you pick them out?

In Figure 7-5, typeface styles and sizes are used inconsistently. One headline is Helvetica 24 point bold; others are Times Roman 18 point bold italic. The body text for one column is 11 point Times Roman; on the other column, it's 10 point Times Roman and 10 point Courier. Column one begins with a widow and ends with an orphan. The contents of the headlines are dull and do not represent the contents of the articles. Some of these things, like mixing typefaces or sizes, can be done artfully. The example above merely shows the mess that can occur if the artfulness is left out. There are few hard and fast rules in design. Figure 7.6 shows what happens when you unify your styles.

FIGURE 7.2 Adding White Space and Graphic Elements

Depository Library Council Report
Restructuring the Depository Library Program

The Fall 1992 Depository Library Council meeting was held Oct 19-20, 1992 in Room LM-407 of the Library of Congress Madison Building. Monday morning was an informal preparatory session for Council, and there were updates from Superintendent of Documents Wayne Kelley and Judy Russell, Director, Library Programs Service.

Staff Changes

Mr. Kelley talked about the various staff changes that have taken place in LPS and Sales. He has asked a dozen mid-level managers to take on new assignments and asked them to take a fresh and inquisitive eye to their areas of new responsibilities to look for ways to improve their performance. The ultimate goal is to implement change to improve GPO's performance and to create an organization that will serve the needs of the American public in the coming years. Judy Russell then reviewed the various staff changes within LPS and what is to be expected as a result of these changes. A comment was made that the community is concerned about these changes. Mr. Kelley said that if these changes resulted in operational problems to please let him know.

Judy also gave an update on the tactical plans for implementing GPO 2001. Tentative drafts are due to the Public Printer by October 30, 1992. The two plans that fall under Mr. Kelley's supervision are: looking at new electronic and print on demand products and services to satisfy customer agency needs and public desires, and development and implementation of electronic capabilities to serve depository libraries. Judy outlined the key points going into their tactical plans (it will probably be one combined plan), and shared some of the critical events they see happening as a result of the plan.

Budgeting

Lastly, Judy gave an update on GPO's budget situation. GPO did a needs-based budget this year, rather than figuring out how to make do with what is appropriated. They came up with $32.5 million requirement and an appropriation of $29 million. It is assumed that since printing and binding is the largest portion of GPO's costs that substantive cuts will have to go there. GPO is looking at a number of alternatives for dealing

with the budget shortfall -- nothing has been finalized at this point.

Remarks of the Public Printer

The formal session began Monday afternoon with opening remarks by Public Printer Robert Houk. He, too, talked about GPO's budget situation. He also mentioned that the appropriations conference report requires the Superintendent of Documents to conduct a study on the feasibility of disseminating information in electronic formats. In doing so, they are to utilize the assistance of the Community College Distant Learning Center in Owensboro, KY. Despite the fact that the WINDO/Gateway bill didn't pass, GPO is moving ahead in an electronic direction. It is not clear that the program structure established 30 years ago is the best possible way to accommodate electronic technology. Which is why Council is looking at restructuring. The purpose of the questions discussed is to transform the DLP into an institution that continues to meet its mission in an era of drastically changing technology, limited funding, and increased public need.

Questions for Council

Question #1 dealt with whether there should be a DLP in the electronic age. How could the program be restructured to fit the realities of the current budget?

Council never came right out and answered this question. Instead it was assumed that there should be a program and Council outlined the goals of such a program. Council later outlined the assumptions it had concerning a restructured program. Assumptions included such things as:

FIGURE 7.3 Bad Design Example #2

PARLIE NEWS

NEWSLETTER OF THE
PHILADELPHIA AREA REFERENCE LIBRARIANS' INFORMATION EXCHANGE

April 1991	Number 67

Meeting Highlights

PARLIE's Winter 1991 meeting on "United States, International and United Nations' Documents" was held on February 28 in Van Pelt Library at the University of Pennsylvania. PARLIE members were joined at the well-attended gathering by members of the Delaware Valley Government Documents Association and the Documents Association of New Jersey.

The opening speaker was Kxxxx Hxxxxxx, Documents Librarian at Penn State, and he spoke on "Using GPO CD-ROM Products." He noted that while these products do offer enhanced searching capability, increased storage capacity and decreased storage space, there are costs as well. CDs bring hardware expenses, installation and maintenance headaches and often come with little or no documentation. Related problems include the variety of non-standardized software used by GPO agencies producing CDs and, in the case of the coming 200+ Census disks, the lack of any software at all.

Appended to Hxxxxxx's presentation was an active Question-and-Answer session which highlighted additional issues: will the technology be outdated 10 years from now? how do you teach patrons how to use several different search interfaces? why is the software for the Congressional Record so bad?

Mxxx Fxxxxx, the Head of Government Publications at the Alexander Library of Rutgers University, followed by describing in detail "Information Sources for International Documents in Reference." Through a series of overheads, she addressed such topics as how to investigate a country, how to locate a UN resolution or a country's voting record and how to learn about UN agencies. Her transparencies spotlighted such sources as US State Department documents, commercial directories (Europa Yearbook for example) and various standard indexes (PAIS, Index to International Statistics, ERIC...).

CONTINUED ON NEXT PAGE

What Can You get for $6?

Where does your $6 PARLIE membership go?

A) It goes to buy lottery tickets for PARLIE Steering Committee members.
B) It goes to buy new suits for Wilson Goode.
C) It's funnelled into a slush fund for the Committee To Reelect President Nixon (CREEPNIX).
D) None of the above.

Unfortunately, "D" is the correct response. As much as we'd like to finance the other worthy causes, we prefer to foolishly squander the money on furthering the progress of PARLIE as a local resource for the professional development of Reference Librarians.

This is done primarily through a series of educational programs, largely featuring speakers from the immediate area. In the past few years, PARLIE has held thought-provoking meetings on such topics as the following:

Government Documents in Reference
(described in this issue)
OCLC's EPIC compared to RLIN
Librarians and Libraries Abroad
Library Management
Publishing and Desktop Publishing
Bibliographic Instruction
CD-ROM Technology
Microcomputers in Libraries
Library Design

These meetings are presented free of charge with complimentary coffee and donuts (if word ever gets out, we'll probably be overrun by policemen on break.) Great care is taken to be as economical as possible, but expenses are unavoidable: the aforementioned coffee and donuts, lunch for the speakers, postage for the newsletter and occasionally travel or honoraria.

CONTINUED ON NEXT PAGE

FIGURE 7.4 Breaking Up an Overly Symmetrical Design

PARLIE NEWS

NEWSLETTER OF THE
PHILADELPHIA AREA REFERENCE LIBRARIANS' INFORMATION EXCHANGE

April 1991   Number 67

Documents and Technology Discussed

PARLIE's Winter 1991 meeting on "United States, International and United Nations' Documents" was held on February 28 in Van Pelt Library at the University of Pennsylvania. PARLIE members were joined at the well-attended gathering by members of the Delaware Valley Government Documents Association and the Documents Association of New Jersey.

The opening speaker was Kxxxx Hxxxxxx, Documents Librarian at Penn State, and he spoke on "Using GPO CD-ROM Products." He noted that while these products do offer enhanced searching capability, increased storage capacity and decreased storage space, there are costs as well. CDs bring hardware expenses, installation and maintenance headaches and often come with little or no documentation. Related problems include the variety of non-standardized software used by GPO agencies producing CDs and, in the case of the coming 200+ Census disks, the lack of any software at all.

Appended to Hxxxxxx's presentation was an active Question-and-Answer session which highlighted additional issues: will the technology be outdated 10 years from now? how do you teach patrons how to use several different search interfaces? why is the software for the Congressional Record so bad?

Mxxx Fxxxxxx, the Head of Government Publications at the Alexander Library of Rutgers University, followed by describing in detail "Information Sources for International Documents in Reference." Through a series of overheads, she addressed such topics as how to investigate a country, how to locate a UN resolution or a country's voting record and how to learn about UN agencies.

Her transparencies spotlighted such sources as US State Department documents, commercial directories (Europa Yearbook for example) and various standard indexes (PAIS, Index to International Statistics, ERIC and so forth).
CONTINUED ON NEXT PAGE

What Can you Get For $6?

Where does your $6 PARLIE membership go?
A) It goes to buy lottery tickets for PARLIE Steering Committee members.
B) It goes to buy new suits for Wilson Goode.
C) It's funnelled into a slush fund for the Committee To Reelect President Nixon (CREEPNIX).
D) None of the above.

Unfortunately, "D" is the correct response. As much as we'd like to finance the other worthy causes, we prefer to foolishly squander the money on furthering the progress of PARLIE as a local resource for the professional development of Reference Librarians.

This is done primarily through a series of educational programs, largely featuring speakers from the immediate area. In the past few years, PARLIE has held thought-provoking meetings on such topics as:
Documents in Reference (see this issue),
OCLC's EPIC compared to RLIN,
Librarians and Libraries Abroad,
Library Management,
Publishing and Desktop Publishing,
Bibliographic Instruction,
CD-ROM Technology,
Microcomputers in Libraries and
Library Design.

These meetings are presented free of charge with complimentary coffee and donuts (if word ever gets out, we'll probably be overrun by policemen on break.) Great care is taken to be as economical as possible, but expenses are unavoidable: the aforementioned coffee and donuts, lunch for the speakers, postage for the newsletter and occasionally travel or honoraria.
CONTINUED ON NEXT PAGE

FIGURE 7.5 Bad Typography Example

PRESIDENT CONT.
available in a New Jersey library.

DANJ is a volunteer organization, and sometimes its members (read: volunteers) cannot devote as much time as they would like to the Association. I know that was true for me during my tenure as President this year. Later this month, I will be compiling the DANJ Annual Report, but already I have received reports from most of the committee and task force chairs. Some of us were able to spend a great deal of time on DANJ activities, while others of us were able only to make small contributions. But our combined achievements contributed to a very successful year for DANJ. I will be sending a copy of the Annual Report to all the 1992 Executive Committee members; if you are not an officer or committee/task force chair and would like a copy, please let me know and I will send it to you.

Finally, I would like to thank you for the opportunity to serve you as DANJ President this year. I am sure you join me in wishing Pxxx Pxxxxxx an even more successful year in 1993, and in offering as much of our time and talents as we can.
-- *Rxxxxx J. Mxxxxx, President, 1992*

STATE DOCUMENT HONORED

Thank you all for your nominations for the first annual State Document of the Year Award. A three member judging panel chose the winning document, <u>Guidelines for the Use and Functioning of Video Display Terminals</u> published by the Public Employees Occupational Safety and Health Program, NJ Department of Health. This well-illustrated document provides a wealth of information regarding video display terminals, especially concerning preventative health measures to be taken by those who work extensively with them. An excellent bibliography is appended for further information. The award was presented at the DANJ Annual Meeting in October. Keep next year's award in mind as you open those depository shipments.
-- *Rxxxxxx Gxxxxxx, Chair, State Documents Task Force*

GODORT NEWS

ALA/GODORT/Council are looking for volunteers. In

Continued on Next Page

GPO CUTBACKS

As many of you may have heard, GPO is reporting that its budget for the next fiscal year is insufficient to cover the costs of running the Depository Library Program. Specifically they have a shortfall of $2.9 million.

In order to meet the shortfall, the Government Printing Office is considering a variety of measures. According to representatives of the GPO, "everything is on the table." At the moment, however, discussion seems to be centering on further conversion of existing print products to microfiche or "other alternative formats." Criteria for the identification of candidates for such conversion include: 1) items selected by a relatively small number of libraries, 2) low content items, such as posters, 3) items where dual distribution (microfiche and paper) already exists, 4) items where duplicative distribution (e.g., more than one paper version) is made, and 5) certain "big ticket" items.

Among the specific titles being discussed are: Code of Federal Regulations, Slip Laws, Slip Opinions, Statutes at Large, U.S. Code, Hearings, Bound Serial Set, Treaties, Index Medicus, Medicare and other manuals.

This proposal to convert such core materials to other formats would have significant impact on those libraries that have chosen to collect them in paper in order to better serve their community.

Those who are concerned about cuts to the program need to make those views known by writing to Robert Houk, the Public Printer.
-- *Rxxxxx L. Oxxxxx,*

ECONOMIC DATA

The New England Electronic Economic Data Center (NEEEDC) offers the Regional Economic Information System (REIS) CD-ROM and the New England Economic Indicators (1969+) online via both a dial-up bulletin board and an Internet FTP file server.

NEEEDC is operated as a public service by the University of Maine and is available 24 hours a day, 7 days a week. The BBS software allows interactive access to the REIS CD-ROM. To access the BBS, have your modem dial (207) 581-1867. To transfer existing files via FTP over the internet, utilize this address: neeedc.umesbs.maine.edu.

FIGURE 7.6 Adding Consistency and Style

PRESIDENT CONT.

DANJ is a volunteer organization, and sometimes its members (read: volunteers) cannot devote as much time as they would like to the Association. I know that was true for me during my tenure as President this year. Later this month, I will be compiling the DANJ Annual Report, but already I have received reports from most of the committee and task force chairs. Some of us were able to spend a great deal of time on DANJ activities, while others of us were able only to make small contributions. But our combined achievements contributed to a very successful year for DANJ. I will be sending a copy of the Annual Report to all the 1992 Executive Committee members; if you are not an officer or committee/task force chair and would like a copy, please let me know and I will send it to you.

Finally, I would like to thank you for the opportunity to serve you as DANJ President this year. I am sure you join me in wishing Pxxx Pxxxxxxxan even more successful year in 1993.

-- Rxxxxxx J. Mxxxxx, President, 1992

NJ Health Dept. Wins State Document Award

Thank you all for your nominations for the first annual State Document of the Year Award. A three member judging panel chose the winning document, <u>Guidelines for the Use and Functioning of Video Display Terminals</u> published by the Public Employees Occupational Safety and Health Program, NJ Department of Health. This well-illustrated document provides a wealth of information regarding video display terminals, especially concerning preventative health measures to be taken by those who work extensively with them. An excellent bibliography is appended for further information. The award was presented at the DANJ Annual Meeting.

-- Rxxxxxx Gxxxxxx, Chair, State Documents Task Force

GODORT Looking for Help

ALA/GODORT/Council are looking for volunteers. In the front of the September issue of <u>Documents to the People</u> there is a list of GODORT positions available. Or you may be interested in having your name or someone else's nominated for Depository Library Council. In either case, contact Rxxxxxx Axxxx Lxxx, Chair, GODORT Nominating Committee (999)999-9999.

GPO Proposes Cutbacks

As many of you may have heard, GPO is reporting that its budget for the next fiscal year is insufficient to cover the costs of running the Depository Library Program. Specifically they have a shortfall of $2.9 million.

In order to meet the shortfall, the Government Printing Office is considering a variety of measures. According to representatives of the GPO, "everything is on the table." At the moment, however, discussion seems to be centering on further conversion of existing print products to microfiche or "other alternative formats." Criteria for the identification of candidates for such conversion include: 1) items selected by a relatively small number of libraries, 2) low content items, such as posters, 3) items where dual distribution (microfiche and paper) already exists, 4) items where duplicative distribution (e.g., more than one paper version) is made, and 5) certain "big ticket" items.

Among the specific titles being discussed are: Code of Federal Regulations, Slip Laws, Slip Opinions, Statutes at Large, U.S. Code, Hearings, Bound Serial Set, Treaties, Index Medicus, Medicare and other manuals.

This proposal to convert such core materials to other formats would have significant impact on those libraries that have chosen to collect them in paper in order to better serve their community.

Those who are concerned about cuts to the program need to make those views known by writing to Robert Houk, the Public Printer.

-- Rxxxxx L. Oxxxxx

Get Free Econ. Data Online

The New England Electronic Economic Data Center (NEEEDC) offers the Regional Economic Information System (REIS) CD-ROM and the New England Economic Indicators (1969+) online via both a dial-up electronic bulletin board and an Internet FTP file server. NEEEDC is operated as a public service by the University of Maine and is available 24 hours a day, 7 days a week. The BBS software allows interactive access to the REIS CD-ROM. To access the BBS, have your modem dial (207) 581-1867. To transfer existing files via FTP over the internet, utilize this address: neeedc.umesbs.maine.edu.

Proofing Checklist for Typographic Elements

- Are the typefaces you have chosen appropriate to this publication? Do the attributes of these typefaces suit the newsletter's audience, message, and writing style?
- Do the typefaces you have chosen fit well together? Are you using too many typefaces?
- Do your type sizes encourage the readability and legibility of your text? Does your word and letter spacing enhance these qualities as well?
- Are you using your chosen typefaces and sizes consistently? Is each headline a certain type style and size? Is the body text consistently expressed in these areas as well? Are your captions and credits consistent? Have you used the styles function of your page-layout program to enforce consistent typographic usage?
- Are there discordant typographic elements that need to be fixed? Do any of your columns begin with a "widow," a short last line of the paragraph begun in a previous column? Do any of your columns end with an "orphan," the first line of a paragraph continued in a following column? If you've used justified text, are there rivers of white space running through your disproportionally spaced text?
- Are your columns too narrow for your typeface so that an excess of hyphens appears to form a ladder on the right side of your columns?
- Is the length of your text columns aligned or irregular? Irregular columns allow you a great deal of freedom, but they may look like they are floating. Aligned columns need to be perfectly aligned to look right.
- Have you used any focal attraction elements? Have you started any articles with drop or stick-up caps? Have you isolated any interesting lines from your stories as pull quotes? Do you have an accurate table of contents? Is there a teaser on your mailer? Are multipage stories connected by jumplines?
- Do your headlines attract attention? Are they large enough? Bold enough? Do they reflect the content of the story in a way that piques the reader's interest?

Look at Figure 7.7 for one last bad example. Check that table. Do the numbers add up? Are they aligned? All of the boxes drawn on this page chop it up too much and rob it of any integrity. The size of the lines drawn on the page is much too black and heavy for the page as well. Aren't there a lot of graphics on this page? Hey, this isn't so hard to fix (see Figure 7.8).

FIGURE 7.7 Bad Graphics Example

DANJ ACTIVITY 1992

REPORT OF THE FEDERAL DOCUMENTS TASK FORCE

During 1992, the FDTF continued to work on designing a training program on U.S. government publications for non-documents librarians. In consultation with Dr. Pxxxxxxx Rxxxxxx at Rutgers SCIS, the Task Force developed an outline of what should be included in a training module. One of Dr. Rxxxxxx's students has created a potential training module which the Task Force plans to review.

Because of the many new challenges for depository librarians created by the large number of CD-ROMs distributed by GPO, the FDTF created a CD-ROM roundtable. The purpose of the roundtable is to provide an opportunity for depository librarians to discuss problems and share ideas about using the new CD-ROMs, and to plan workshops on installing and using these products.

Respectfully submitted,
Dxxxxx F. Hxxx, Chair, 1992

REPORT OF THE INTERNATIONAL AND FOREIGN DOCUMENTS TASK FORCE

Princeton University's Firestone Library was the site of a May 22 IFDTF meeting at which time attendees focused on problems involving the acquisition of international documents. The demise of International Bibliography during the spring of 1992 exacerbates the selection and acquisition process for many libraries, and discussion centered on ways to bridge this gap. The Task Force authorized the chair to request consideration of the matter at the ALA convention in San Francisco, and it was subsequently placed on the agenda of the GODORT/IDTF's meetings. (Following discussion at the IDTF business and steering committee meetings at the ALA annual convention, GODORT authorized the drafting of a letter to CIS to see if they might be interested in providing a product to fill our needs and offering IDTF's assistance in suggesting what was most useful in the former publication and what our needs actually are.)

Following the business portion of the May 22 meeting, Sxxxx Wxxxx provided attendees with a demonstration of the Readex Index to United Nations Documents and Publications on CD-ROM and a tour of Princeton's United Nations collection

Respectfully submitted,
Mxxx Fxxxxx, Chair, 1992

REPORT OF THE STATE DOCUMENTS TASK FORCE

The Task Force began a pilot program for PALS, the state agency liaison program. The PALS coordinator, Rxxxxx Mxxxxx, and another DANJ volunteer, Axxx Mxxxx Jxx, have been working with the Atlantic City Convention Authority and Expressway Authority and the Office of State Planning. Rxxxxxx Gxxxxxx gave an overview of the program at the DANJ Annual Conference in October.

Nomination forms for the first annual State Document of the Year Award were sent out to all N.J. state document depository libraries through the N.J. depository shipments in the spring. A three-member judging panel chose the winning document: <u>Guidelines for the Use and Functioning of Video Display Terminals</u>, put out by the Public Employees Occupational Safety and Health Program, N.J. Department of Health. The award was presented at the DANJ Annual Conference in October.

The Task Force visited the State Library where Bxx Lxxx gave a tour of the State Depository System.

The Task Force's primary goals for 1993 are to continue working on the issue of permanent paper for state documents and adding at least three more agencies to the PALS program. Rxxxxxx Gxxxxxx will continue as chair of the Task Force for 1993.

Respectfully submitted,
Rxxxxxx Gxxxxxx, Chair, 1992

TREASURER'S REPORT 2/4/92

DANJ TREASURY CURRENT BALANCE $2626.31

1992 Budget Projections
  Income

Checking Account Interest (est.)	$ 100.00
Membership Dues (est.)	$ 400.00
Subtotal:	$ 500.00

Expenditures

DANJ Newsletter (est.)	$ 986.00
Membership Mailings (est.)	$ 131.00
Annual State Incorporation Fee	$ 15.00
DANJ Dues NJ Law Librarians	$ 10.00
Grant Program Award	$ 500.00
State Notable Document Award	$ 100.00
Task Forces (4)/Committees (2)	$ 150.00
Subtotal:	$1892.00
Net Loss:	**$[1292.00]**

PROJECTED BALANCE 12/31/92 $1234.31
-- Exxx Cxxxxxx, Treasurer

FIGURE 7.8 Lightening and Unbinding the Page

Preeeesenting... DANJ ACTIVITY 1992

Federal Documents Task Force

During 1992, the FDTF continued to work on designing a training program on U.S. government publications for nondocuments librarians. In consultation with Dr. Pxxxxxx Rxxxxxx at Rutgers SCIS, the Task Force developed an outline of what should be included in a training module. One of Dr. Rxxxxxx's students has created a potential training module which the Task Force plans to review.

Because of the many new challenges for depository librarians created by the large number of CD-ROMs distributed by GPO, the FDTF created a CD-ROM roundtable. The purpose of the roundtable is to provide an opportunity for depository librarians to discuss problems and share ideas about using the new CD-ROMs, and to plan workshops on installing and using these products.

Respectfully submitted,
Dxxxx F. Hxxx, Chair, 1992

International and Foreign Documents Task Force

Princeton University's Firestone Library was the site of a May 22 IFDTF meeting at which time attendees focused on problems involving the acquisition of international documents. The demise of International Bibliography during the spring of 1992 exacerbates the selection and acquisition process for many libraries, and discussion centered on ways to bridge this gap. The Task Force authorized the chair to request consideration of the matter at the ALA convention in San Francisco, and it was subsequently placed on the agenda of the GODORT/IDTF's meetings. (Following discussion at the IDTF business and steering committee meetings at the ALA annual convention, GODORT authorized the drafting of a letter to CIS to see if they might be interested in providing a product to fill our needs and offering IDTF's assistance in suggesting what was most useful in the former publication and what our needs actually are.)

Following the business portion of the May 22 meeting, Sxxxx Wxxxx provided attendees with a demonstration of the Readex Index to United Nations Documents and Publications on CD-ROM and a tour of Princeton's United Nations collection

Respectfully submitted,
Mxxx Fxxxxx, Chair, 1992

State Documents Task Force

The Task Force began a pilot program for PALS, the state agency liaison program. The PALS coordinator, Rxxxxx Mxxxxx, and another DANJ volunteer, Axxx Mxxxxx Jxx, have been working with the Atlantic City Convention Authority and Expressway Authority and the Office of State Planning. Rxxxxxx Gxxxxxx gave an overview of the program at the DANJ Annual Conference in October.

Nomination forms for the first annual State Document of the Year Award were sent out to all N.J. state document depository libraries through the N.J. depository shipments in the spring. A three-member judging panel chose the winning document: Guidelines for the Use and Functioning of Video Display Terminals, put out by the Public Employees Occupational Safety and Health Program, N.J. Department of Health. The award was presented at the DANJ Annual Conference in October.

The Task Force visited the State Library where Bxx Lxxx gave a tour of the State Depository System.

The Task Force's primary goals for 1993 are to continue working on the issue of permanent paper for state documents and adding at least three more agencies to the PALS program. Rxxxxxx Gxxxxxx will continue as chair of the Task Force for 1993.

Respectfully submitted,
Rxxxxxx Gxxxxxx, Chair, 1992

Treasurer's Report 2/4/92

DANJ Treasury Current Balance		$2626.31
1992 Budget Projections		
Income		
Checking Account Interest (est.)		$ 100.00
Membership Dues (est.)		$ 400.00
Subtotal:		$ 500.00
Expenditures		
DANJ Newsletter (est.)		$ 986.00
Membership Mailings (est.)		$ 131.00
Annual State Incorporation Fee		$ 15.00
DANJ Dues NJ Law Librarians		$ 10.00
Grant Program Award		$ 500.00
State Notable Document Award		$ 100.00
Task Forces (4)/Committees (2)		$ 150.00
Subtotal:		$1892.00
Net Loss:		$[1392.00]
Projected Balance	12/31/92	$1234.31

-- Exxxx Cxxxxxx, Treasurer

Proofing Checklist for the Use of Graphics

- Is the nameplate of your newsletter properly aligned? Is it noticeable, distinctive, and appealing?
- Do your visual images augment the content of the text? Do they add to the overall message of the publication?
- Are your photographs, illustrations, or clip art cropped so that there are no non-essential elements to each image? Are they sized so that they neither control the page by being too large nor get lost on it by being too small? Are they in alignment with each other and the text?
- Are your charts and graphs drawn accurately? Are they labeled accurately? Do the numbers add up correctly? Do the charts and graphs enhance the message of the text? Are they aligned with the text and other graphics on the page? Is the labeling properly aligned within the charts and graphs?
- Have you used boxes and tinted screens sparsely but effectively to highlight important parts of your page?
- Have you used rules as barriers to break up white space and to distinguish between different page elements? Are your rules drawn with too dark a point size so that they weigh down the page?
- Are the conclusions of your articles noted by an end-of-story sign?
- Is there no more than one dominant image on each page or on each two-page spread? Does this dominant image reflect the content of the text? Does it convey the most important idea your text is trying to convey?

PRINT OPTIONS

Finally, your pages are just the way you want them, and you are ready to have them printed. You now have three main options: (1) You can take the printed masters to a print or photocopy shop and have them photocopied, collated, and perhaps stapled. (2) You can take the printed masters to a print shop and have the printer make a master plate from it to produce copies on their printer using ink. (3) You can take your publication to your print shop as a file on a disk or send it to them via modem or even the Internet if they have those capabilities, and the printer will print your newsletter direct from its digital representation. From option one to option three, both the costs and quality increase significantly.

Certainly for most library house organs, and even for many librarian professional connection newsletters, photocopy quality is sufficient as long as you choose a good photocopy shop. For library publicity vehicles and for any newsletter that will be using photographs, complex images, or color, professional printing is the better choice.

Photocopiers reproduce from the 300–600 dots-per-inch resolution produced by the typical laser printer; a printing press provides higher quality reproduction. Printers can also bleed to the very edge of the page and can handle four-color separations. If you opt for a printer and are sending them disks, make sure that your page-layout files are compatible with the print shop's operation. Check with a number of different printers and compare cost estimates and quality. To compare quality, have some test files printed. Test files should contain the typefaces, type styles, and sizes you normally use as well as sample rules, boxes, and tints. If you will be working with clip art, photographs, or scanned images, include an example or two of typical visuals as well. Allow yourself time to choose a printer you feel comfortable with; it could be a long-term relationship.

Even if you are having your master pages photocopied, you need to compare. Costs and quality vary among photocopy shops as well. Follow the same procedures you would in selecting a printer. Get price estimates, have some test pages copied, and choose a copy shop you are comfortable with. Of course, with many institutions you will not have a choice. You'll have any copying or printing done in-house. If so, try to cultivate a good working relationship with your friends at the in-house print shop. You will need their cooperation.

THE WEB

An additional or supplemental publishing alternative is the World Wide Web (WWW). This alternative is fully discussed in section 4, which covers the creation of WWW home pages. One of the connections or links from that organizational home page could be a repository for the organization's newsletter. To what extent the newsletter is mounted is entirely up to the organization. The easiest way is to simply mount the text of the articles, or even just the text of the most significant articles. Graphics could be included, but the layout would be completely different because of the peculiarities of the Web (as can be seen in section 4). Links to related Web sites could be added. Essentially, to proceed in this manner would require the newsletter to be completely redesigned to maximize WWW utility.

Another option is to convert the newsletter file into a document format like Adobe Acrobat's Portable Document Format (PDF). In this format, each page of the newsletter retains the look of the original and cannot be edited. These methods may be more than you want to tackle, but, as previously noted, merely uploading newsletter text files and making them accessible from an organizational home page is a simple proposition that could greatly enhance your distribution possibilities.

DISTRIBUTION OPTIONS

How your newsletter will be distributed depends on the type of newsletter. A library house organ or librarian's professional connection will be distributed along membership lines. Employees will receive their house organ through interoffice mail; members will receive their professional connection through the U.S. mail.

Publicity vehicles can be distributed passively or aggressively. The passive approach is to leave stacks of the publications in prominent places, free to all takers. These locations should be placed where your target audience can be expected to pass by in a reasonably attentive state. A passive approach is fine as a supplement to a more aggressive one, but depending on your audience as a whole to find your newsletter is relying too strongly on the kindness of strangers. You have to grab your readers just as your design must grab their attention. An aggressive approach is a mailing list. Send your publicity vehicle to all faculty, or to all residents, or to all partners in a firm, or to whomever your audience may be.

In most of these distribution methods, the U.S. mail figures prominently. Even with the postal service, you have a choice: stamps or bulk mail permit. A bulk mail permit gives you a slight break in the price per item, but the paperwork for the application and the regulations to maintain the working agreement are daunting. You don't use stamps, but instead a postage meter to pay postage rates. You also pay an annual bulk mail fee. Each mailing must have a minimum of 200 pieces, each not weighing more than 16 ounces. Your metered mail must be sorted by zip code and bundled by special post office–approved rubber bands in the proper post office sacks. Bulk mail must be second, third, or fourth class mail and will not be forwarded or returned to sender. Unless you have a mail room to handle all of this, that's a very small payoff for not using stamps.

If you use self-adhesive stamps, which you don't have to wet to affix, then your mailing process is easy. Print out a set of mailing labels or have the maintainer of the organization's membership database do so. Affix a label and stamp to each newsletter. Deposit the whole batch in any mail box or post office. And you'll probably have some dealings with your organization's treasurer in order to get reimbursed for such expenses as stamps and printing. The ease of those procedures will vary with each organization.

Your newsletter is done. You've planned your overall design and implemented it with a compelling mix of text, graphics, and white space. You've communicated your message to a selected audience in the style best suited to both the message and the audience. One issue is published. Now start planning your next issue. How can you make it better?

SECTION 3
LIBRARY GUIDES

8 INFO TO GO: PLANNING LIBRARY GUIDES

Walk into any library, and you'll find that library guides encompass many different printed materials. Although their content, appearance, and form differ considerably, library guides are used in all types of libraries. A library guide might be a subject bibliography, a point-of-use guide detailing the best way to use a particular resource, a brochure about the library and its rules and regulations, a description of a library collection or service (like interlibrary loan), a self-guided tour, a map of the building, a flyer for a library program, a calendar of upcoming events, ready reference material on an oft-requested topic (like how to record bibliographic citations), or an entire library handbook listing library policies, departments, and directory information. Even the lowly bookmark can be considered a library guide if it contains some useful information regarding library hours or policies.

"Some useful information" is the key. If you've been drafted to write one or a whole series of guides, you'll soon realize that what all library guides have in common is an educational message. The content and display of that message vary to the extremes described above. In this chapter and the next, the focus will be primarily on two types of library guides: bibliographies and point-of-use guides. These two can be broken down into a number of subcategories.

BIBLIOGRAPHIES

Bibliographies can be assembled for a variety of purposes and audiences. They might focus on only books, or they could include periodicals, indexes, online sources, and other media. They might be restricted to reference books such as handbooks and directories, or they might give an overview of an entire subject in the form of a pathfinder. They might be devised for a particular class at an academic institution, or they might spotlight specific books and other materials public libraries think their patrons will enjoy or ask about frequently.

A booklist is a short, select list of books that have some common ground. Generally, it lists books on a topic popular with the patrons of that library, whether it be mystery novels, presidential biographies, or books for young adults. However, booklists are also created for new books and for topics the library wishes to highlight like "unsung women in history" or "great library fundraising schemes." They may be annotated and may have a limited shelf life depending on the timeliness of the topic.

Pathfinders are a more systematic approach to educating library users about library resources. Pathfinders typically include an introductory "scope note," where the topic is defined and terminology is explained. Relevant subject headings for the catalog may be included as well, even if your online catalog allows for keyword searching. A small selection of classic books on the topic is listed, as are special reference materials such as handbooks and subject encyclopedias. Published subject bibliographies should have their own section in the pathfinder. Periodical indexes and abstracts related to the subject will be listed also. Proceedings, reports, online resources, and other media may warrant their own sections depending on the topic and available materials.

Course-related bibliographies are often distributed in bibliographic instruction sessions and are usually devoted to resources useful in completing the assignments for a particular class. They list the reference and reserve materials as well as periodical indexes and abstracts most appropriate to the subject covered in a specific class. Course-related bibliographies can also be designed more broadly to list resources for a group of related courses, or they might be focused more narrowly on resources for certain assignments within a course.

Another way to construct a course-related bibliography is to take a search-strategy approach rather than to simply list resources by categories, e.g., encyclopedias, indexes, reference books. A search-strategy approach focuses on the process of research as would a pathfinder. It emphasizes how to find information to answer types of questions. Rather than listing periodical information under "Indexes and Abstracts," a search strategy approach might list it under "How to Find Journal Articles on Your Topic." It's a simple change, but it can make your bibliography more relevant to the typical library user who may be discouraged by library jargon.

POINT-OF-USE GUIDES

Point-of-use materials take a process-oriented approach, because that's exactly what they are doing: describing a process, how to use something. Point-of-use materials can be in the form of handouts, posters, or charts and are kept in close proximity to the research tool they are explaining. They have been helpful for many years in explaining difficult printed reference tools like *Chemical Abstracts* or *Social Science Citation Index*, but it was with the expanded use of computers that point-of-use materials became prevalent. They are designed to explain complex tools and, considering the variety of software interfaces for searchable databases accessible in libraries, are much needed in today's library. They also cut down on staff time spent explaining every detail of a resource to every patron.

Point-of-use materials are essentially compact procedures manuals. Many of the computer databases for which librarians devise point-of-use materials come with complete user manuals written by the product's vendor, but most users don't want to wade through all that detail to find out how to search the database and display the results. Frequently, vendors even supply point-of-use guides of their own, but librarians may still prefer to create their own guides tailored to the needs of the library's users, and to include information (such as policies or locations) specific to that library.

BEGINNING TO PLAN

Once you've decided which type of guide you're going to produce, it's time to target your audience, define your message, and clarify your instructional goals and objectives.

FINDING YOUR AUDIENCE

When planning a library guide, you need to ask the same first question you would when planning a newsletter: Who is your audience? With this library guide, are you trying to reach every person who walks through the front door, every user who dials up your online catalog from home, or a specific subset of the larger group? Do the various people in your projected audience have different levels of understanding of libraries, English, or computers; or are there any other factors bearing on the information in this guide? Are you aiming at high school students, college freshmen, students in a particular class, or professionals? Is your target a broader group of those needing information about a subject who are not likely to ask for help? Are you writing for those who use the library when no one in public service is available to help? How you answer these questions will impact the tone of your writing, the content of the guide, the organization of the information, and the format and layout of the page.

DEFINING YOUR MESSAGE

No matter what type of library guide (or publication) you are planning, you need to define the message you are trying to convey. With library guides, your message will be educational; you are presenting information the user needs to locate materials or services or to use specific tools. Regardless of the topic, the object must be to benefit the user and to provide needed information in a usable format. A bibliography should include the resources most useful to the targeted audience. A point-of-use guide must outline the most desired functions of a particular tool. And both must be appropriate in language and format to the user's learning style.

Bibliographies and point-of-use materials are generally organized in divergent ways, because they are generally used very differently. A bibliography is a reference document that does not need to be read sequentially. You would not read a dictionary from A to Z, and neither would you read a bibliography like a novel. Even if your bibliography takes a search-strategy approach, the user is likely to focus on what he or she needs right now (how to find journal articles or how to find statistics, for example.)

A point-of-use guide, however, is written to be read sequentially. First you do this, then this, then that happens, and you do this. Once the user has learned the tool described by the guide, the guide may be retained as a reference that is not used strictly in sequence as a whole, but that still might be used that way in part. For instance, you may remember how to search the system, but forget how to download the records to your disk. You would not read the sections of the guide dealing with searching the database, but would skip to the section on downloading. You then would read that section step by step in order to get the process right.

CLARIFYING YOUR INSTRUCTIONAL GOALS AND OBJECTIVES

Both types of guides are used as instructional devices, and in planning a library guide it is good to keep instructional goals and objectives in mind. What should the user be able to do after reading this guide? Search the catalog using subject headings? Search the catalog using keywords? Search the catalog and be able to successfully interpret the item information for each record retrieved? Limit a search to a range of publication years? Formulate a search strategy? Select the appropriate library database and search it for relevant articles? Be able to mark and then print or download those records? Be able to identify which articles are in journals owned by the library?

You may find that you are trying to combine too many objectives into one guide, and that it is better to divide the planned single guide into two guides. The different skills levels of your projected users will further complicate this process. Do you need a basic guide for novices and an advanced guide for experienced users? Do you need a basic bibliography for freshmen and a more detailed one for graduate students?

However these questions are answered, certain guidelines apply. Keep it simple; don't try to cram too many words on a page or too many concepts into a guide, whether your audience is primarily made up of beginners or skilled researchers. Most users will tend to scan written guides as quickly as possible—which gives you another reason to limit what you are trying to convey. At the same time, someone who picks up a guide is interested in the topic, so you have a potentially receptive audience to your message if you can hold its attention.

Guides need to be readable and to feature both clear language and uncluttered layout. They need to be concise, accurate, and free of jargon. The tone and format should be suitable to the target audience. Each guide should be recognizable as part of the library's series of materials, and its purpose should be readily identifiable. Each guide should be easy to read and use.

Bad guides try to transmit too much information; instead of providing instruction, they provide frustration. Always realize that a written guide is intended to stand on its own. While it is a good idea to note how and when additional in-person help is available, the written guide should be designed so that users can attain certain instructional objectives on their own. There may not be anyone around to ask questions of when the user is reading the guide. Use simple terms, short sentences and compact paragraphs. Your diction should not cause any friction.

It is better not to attempt teaching complex concepts in a guide. A bibliography will get users started on where to look for information, but it will not help the user evaluate which sources are better for investigating a specific question. There is also doubt about how transferable research knowledge is. Guide A outlines how to find information on Topic A. Can the user then transfer those research methods to Topic B? Some can, and some cannot. Finally, to be useful, written guides need to be revised and updated fairly frequently. Is maintenance a part of your total plan for instructional guides?

A COMPREHENSIVE PLAN

It is important to remember that although you may be writing only one library guide at a time, it is not the only guide your library will be publishing. Whether you are writing all the guides for the library or are writing some and editing others, you need to consider each one as part of a related series. Should there be a standardized logo or format? How many guides? How many pages per guide? How many copies of each guide? These questions need to be addressed not only in terms of who your audience is and what information you need to convey, but also in terms of how large your budget is. These questions can also affect how much you try to convey in each guide, but be careful not to try to fit too much in each one. That will only detract from the quality of the materials. Guides should be designed on a basis of user needs/user benefits as determined by the library staff from their dealings with the public.

The usual technical questions apply. What kind of paper? Where will the guide be printed or copied? How will it be distributed? Although these questions are important, they are likely to have been standardized by the time you get involved. Guides are probably copied by the in-house or local printer who does all the institution's work. Distribution is likely to be via a display rack in the library building and possibly on a website.

Library guides do need to be considered part of the library's instructional program. As such they need to fit in with instructional classes and outreach efforts conducted by the library. They need to be tested, evaluated, and regularly updated. They should be devised, or at least edited, with the whole series in mind.

QUESTIONS OF DESIGN

The design or layout of each library guide should be consistent with all other guides published by the library. It is likely that you will be using a one-column grid for your layout (see Figure 8.1), although a simple, asymmetrical, two-column design gives you a wide column for body text and a narrow column for headings or annotations and gives the page ample white space (see Figure 8.2). In either case, you will not be attempting any of the more flashy and complicated layouts discussed in the section on newsletters. The layout needs to be distinctive, attractive, and, above all, clear.

Certain basic rules of typography also need to be followed. Choose the right typeface to connote the personality you want the guide to express, and stick to just one or two typefaces for

FIGURE 8.1 One-Column Layout for a Library Guide

ROBESON LIBRARY
RUTGERS UNIVERSITY

USING PSYCLIT

INFO
GUIDE

FORM A SEARCH STRATEGY

1. Summarize your topic into a short statement.
2. Underline the main concepts.
3. List the related terms which express these concepts. (One way to find related terms is to use the thesaurus for your database.)
4. Write out your strategy combining the terms as described below.

   Use **AND** to find records which contain both term A and term B. This narrows the search.
   FIND: CREATIVITY AND CHILDREN (will find citations which include both "creativity" and "children.")
   Use **OR** to find records that contain either A or B. This broadens the search.
   FIND: TEACHING OR INSTRUCTION (will find citations which include either "teaching" or "instruction.")

SEARCH THE DATABASE

1. From the on-screen menu which lists the available databases, type "A"and press RETURN or ENTER.
2. When the FIND prompt appears at the bottom of the screen, type in the term or terms you wish to find (see *Form A Search Strategy* above) and press RETURN or ENTER. (At any time you may press the **F2** key to return to the search prompt and enter new search terms. The Function keys are either at the left of the keyboard or across the top of the keyboard.)

   The number of bibliographic records containing the terms you selected will be indicated on the screen.

SEARCH IN SPECIFIC FIELDS

You can also search for terms which appear in particular fields in the record to increase the specificity of your search. Examples are given below.

FIELD NAMES	SEARCH EXAMPLES	SAMPLE RECORD
Title	Literacy in TI	TI: Acquisition of literary; children in first grade
Author	Juel-Connie in AU	AU: Juel-Connie
Journal Name	Journal-of-educational-psychology in JN	JN: Journal-of-Educational-Psychology; 1986 Aug Vol 78(4) 243-255
Language	English in LA	LA: English
Publication Year	1986 in PY or PY=1986	PY: 1986
Descriptor	Reading-comprehension in de	DE: READING-COMPREHENSION; SCHOOL-AGE-CHILDREN

VIEW THE RESULTS

1. Press the **F4** key. The system will show you the first record.
2. Use the PgDn or PgUp keys to move through the record.
   To see the next record, press **Ctrl** and hit **PgDn**. To see the previous record, press **Ctrl** and hit **PgUp**.
3. To mark specific records to download, press "**M**". To unmark a record, press "**U**".

DOWNLOAD OR TRANSFER RECORDS

You can put all the records you want on a diskette so that you can work with them using other software.

1) Insert a DOS-formatted 5 1/4" floppy diskette in the PC disk drive.
2) Press the **F10** key and then "**D**." Now hit "**S**" to start downloading.

FIGURE 8.2 Two-Column Layout for a Library Guide

ROBESON LIBRARY
RUTGERS UNIVERSITY
USING PSYCLIT
INFO
GUIDE

**Form a
Search
Strategy**

1. Summarize your topic into a short statement.
2. Underline the main concepts.
3. List the related terms which express these concepts. (One way to find related terms is to use the thesaurus for your database.)
4. Write out your strategy combining the terms as described below.

Use **AND** to find records which contain both term A and term B. This narrows the search.
   FIND: CREATIVITY AND CHILDREN (will find citations which include both "creativity" and "children.")
Use **OR** to find records that contain either A or B. This broadens the search.
   FIND: TEACHING OR INSTRUCTION (will find citations which include either "teaching" or "instruction.")

**Search the
Database**

1. From the on-screen menu which lists the available databases, type "A" and press RETURN or ENTER.
2. When the FIND prompt appears at the bottom of the screen, type in the term or terms you wish to find (see *Form A Search Strategy* above) and press RETURN or ENTER. (At any time you may press the **F2** key to return to the search prompt and enter new search terms. The Function keys are either at the left of the keyboard or across the top of the keyboard.)

The number of bibliographic records containing the terms you selected will be indicated on the screen.

**Search in
Specific
Fields**

You can also search for terms which appear in particular fields in the record to increase the specificity of your search. Examples are given below.

Field Names	*Search Examples*	*Sample Record*
Title	Literacy in TI	TI: Acquisition of literary; children in first grade
Author	Juel-Connie in AU	AU: Juel-Connie
Journal Name	Journal-of-educational-psychology	JN: Journal-of-Educational-Psychology 1986 Aug Vol 78(4) 243-255
Language	English in LA	LA: English
Publication Year	1986 in PY or PY=1986	PY: 1986
Descriptor	Reading-comprehension in de	DE: READING-COMPREHENSION; SCHOOL-AGE-CHILDREN

**View the
Results**

1. Press the **F4** key. The system will show you the first record.
2. Use the PgDn or PgUp keys to move through the record. To see the next record, press **Ctrl** and hit **PgDn**. To see the previous record, press **Ctrl** and hit **PgUp.**
3. To mark specific records to download, press "**M**". To unmark a record, press "**U**".

**Download or
Transfer
Records**

You can put all the records you want on a diskette so that you can work with them using other software.

1) Insert a DOS-formatted 5 1/4" floppy diskette in the PC disk drive.
2) Press the **F10** key and then "**D.**" Now hit "**S**" to start downloading.

this and all other guides you have planned. As with newsletters, the details of these overall typographic decisions can be outlined in a style sheet so it is you can implement your choices consistently. Make sure the point size is large enough to be read easily. Don't rely on all capital letters for emphasis. Using all capitals does grab attention, because it looks like the writer is yelling at the reader, but for more than two or three words, they are more difficult to read. Typographic emphasis is better achieved with boldface and italics. Tabs and indents can also be useful here. Underlining is less attractive and should be used sparingly.

White space is important, so mind your leading and word and character spacing. Ragged right usually works better in the simple layouts used by library guides, which feature short choppy text blocks, but justified text can be used if you prefer. Be consistent in how you use terms, names, abbreviations, and numbers. Finally, make sure spelling and punctuation are correct because those mistakes tend to leap out at the reader.

ORGANIZATION

Perhaps the most significant decision you must make in planning a library guide is how to organize your content, which will depend to a certain extent upon the type of information to be transmitted. A point-of-use guide most likely will be arranged according to a chronology of procedural steps (first, you do this, then that). However, a point-of-use guide might be arranged according to cause and effect criteria (if you want to see this, then you must do that). Or a chronologically arranged, step-by-step guide might have a troubleshooting section arranged by cause and effect.

A bibliography might be arranged according to either physical or logical location (Reference Books, then Government Documents). It also might be arranged by a quantifiable hierarchy in either ascending or descending order (most important works, then less important ones). Or a combination of the two is possible (most important reference books, then less important reference books, then most important government documents, and so forth). You could also arrange a bibliography by cause and effect (if you want information on X, look in this book). You would not arrange a bibliography by chronology, nor would you arrange a point-of-use guide by location or hierarchy.

The cause-and-effect approach is also useful for a compilation of library rules and regulations, while the location arrangement is ideally suited for floorplans and maps. A hierarchy is the best arrangement of a glossary of terminology.

A FORMAT FOR YOUR LAYOUT

Once you have worked out the order in which information will be listed, you need to devise a system of page formatting that will best present it. Your margins and line spacing should allow for enough white space so that the text is easily read and is pleasing in appearance. Different sections of the guide are best delineated with white space, headings, and subheadings. Additional tools to divide the page include step numbers, outlining indents, paragraphs, lines, boxes, and other graphical elements. As was described in previous chapters, working with these sorts of elements is easy enough with desktop publishing. The difficult part is using everything in balance.

Furthermore, use all these page formatting tools consistently within both this particular guide and all other guides for your library. If you indicate a new heading with a double space on the first page of the guide, then you need to do so on the second page, too. And you should use that same spacing to indicate heading changes on other library guides as well. In short, page formatting will require a style sheet in order to maintain consistency.

Desktop publishing permits you to incorporate illustrations and other graphics easily. Illustrations are often used in the nameplate of library guides, usually in the form of the logo of the library or parent organization. This gives the library's publications a distinctive, identifiable look and can add a great deal to the appearance of the guide as long as the logo is attractive.

Illustrations, tables, charts, and graphs in library guides can also complement the content of the text. Often the reader can better understand a complicated database interface if some screen captures from the database are provided. Screen-capture programs are available commercially and as shareware that allow you to import screens directly into your page-layout program or perhaps even your word processor so you can improve the clarity of the guide. All of the usual rules of using graphics apply, of course. The graphic should be relevant and should be located on the page near the related text. The graphic should be large enough to be seen clearly, but not so large as to dwarf the other elements on the page. Graphics should be clearly labeled and should fit with the tone of the publication.

If you are planning on using color to accent parts of your guides, do so with caution. Remember that some of your users are color blind, and that colored inks can be more difficult to read than the traditional black. If you are planning on using colored paper, make sure that it is light enough for text to be clearly legible for those with less than perfect eyesight. As long as you keep legibility in mind, colored paper can be an excellent organizing principle. You might use one color for point-of-use guides, another for bibliographies, a third for policy- and service-related guides, and so on. Just make sure that your words can be easily read and understood.

By all means, look at the guides of other libraries when planning your own. Don't be afraid to appropriate a well-executed design and tailor it to your library's needs. The Library Orientation/Instruction Exchange (LOEX) at Eastern Michigan University has scores of instructional materials on hand. These can be borrowed and studied by members. But what you create for your library should be unique, because your users and their needs are unique. Using desktop publishing to create handsome library guides can help fill those needs.

GETTING THE WORD OUT: PRODUCING AND PUBLISHING LIBRARY GUIDES

With newsletters, design and layout comprise approximately one-half of the process. Content is the driving force and raison d'être, but layout demands a great deal of production time in desktop publishing. Library guides differ from this model.

Since library guides are driven by content to an even greater extent than are most newsletters, viable layout options are far fewer; the key is to find a simple overall design for your series of guides and to stick with it. You are not looking to make a big splash with your design; your main concern is that the design make the content easy to read. You are conveying essential information on a topic chosen for its interest to your readers; you want your readers to focus entirely on that information and not on an overly clever design. Of course, the design still must be attractive enough to get and hold your audience's attention.

Because of this difference in the relative value of design to the publication, a page-layout package is much less necessary to produce a nice guide than it is to produce an eye-catching newsletter. Your layout is likely to be so simple that a good word processor can do the job very well. If you have a page-layout program, then by all means use it. It puts many layout tools at your fingertips, but don't purchase one simply to create library guides.

INFORMATION GATHERING

As indicated in chapter 8, our focus is on two types of library guides: the bibliography and the point-of-use guide. The production process for both starts with information gathering or research. For a bibliography, the research question is simple: What resources on this topic would be most useful to the users of this guide? As librarians, bibliographic research is what we have been trained to do and what we do on an on-demand basis at the reference desk every day. Think like a reference librarian does when answering a reference question, and consider the knowledge and abilities of your user. Choose resources that are at the user's level and that provide the type of information most needed.

How do you know what level and type of information the user will want? If you are in an academic institution, contact with students and faculty will give you the answers. That is especially true for bibliographies geared to specific courses. For public and special libraries, the answer is with the users. If for some reason you don't have an opportunity to interact with them, then discuss the needs of your users with colleagues who do. The bibliography is intended to benefit the users and not be a piece of exquisite scholarship that does not fill a local need.

Point-of-use materials are compressed manuals. The object is to teach a reader how to use a particular resource. That resource may be a printed index, a computer database, an automated book checkout system, or any resource that your patrons may have difficulty using by themselves. Your guide must provide the information the user needs to use the resource effectively. However, the user does not want to read a manual, and you do not have to include everything you know about the resource. Remember, this is meant to be a compressed manual. Information is included on a need-to-know basis.

You must use the resource yourself, take notes, and create an outline. Don't rely on an in-depth manual provided by the vendor of the product. Manuals can be wrong, incomplete, or misleading. You want your guide to be fully accurate and clear, so you must put your hands on the product. While you should learn the resource thoroughly, what you will include in the guide are its most important features and perhaps their limitations. You need to keep in mind what users will want to get from this resource and in what form they will want that result. The content of your guide should be tailored accordingly.

Very few people enjoy reading manuals or extended guides. Your users want to see clear, concise instructions on how to get what they want as quickly and easily as possible. Do your hands-on research with that objective in mind, and organize what you learn in a detailed outline.

WRITING

Writing has at least two steps, drafting and editing. These two are often followed by more editing and still more editing. What you are trying to accomplish with the draft, however, is to record your words in some organized fashion with as little delay as possible. Once saved as a word processing file, your text is easily manipulated, edited, and completely rewritten if necessary. One would think that the ease with which text can be drastically edited today would have led to widespread improvement of written expression. Judging the written evidence encountered in everyday life, this hasn't occurred. Bad writing flourishes, and one reason is that too often writers mistake drafting for writing, and editing for copyediting. Shakespeare is dead. Take a close look at what you've written; it could probably stand some revision.

Good organization is a quality common to the best bibliographies and point-of-use materials so when drafting your guide, pay attention to the organization of your information. Is the information laid out so that users will look for it? Does the organization of your text mirror how most users will, or should, approach research on this topic?

Because there is little actual writing in a library guide bibliography, additional writing concerns are less critical to their success. Point-of-use materials, however, need to be concerned with the quality of the writing. Whether it be friendly and informal or practical and formal, make sure your tone is the one you want to use. Is the tone consistent throughout the guide or guides? Are you using language that users are likely to understand? Wordiness and complex diction are enemies to clear writing, and that is particularly significant when writing instructions. Avoid the use of jargon—words that refer to terms from the library world, terms specific to a certain discipline, or "computerese." Users may not know what a "bibliographic record" is, for example. Find layman's synonyms for jargon whenever possible. Are your sentences simple and direct? They need not be all as short as those in a Dick and Jane reading primer, but the ideas in each sentence need to be clearly expressed. Are your titles and/or headlines brief and clear? Do they accurately describe the text that follows?

That text is made up of words. Above all, those words need to be intelligible and concise in their expression. Don't say, "The optimum method to facilitate research of monographs is to use Brunhilda, the library's Online Public Access Catalog (OPAC)." Instead say, "To find books, use the online catalog."

For most writing, an active voice is preferred. Point-of-use materials, which rely heavily on step-by-step commands, are no exception. Don't say, "In order to find an article, the index must be consulted." Instead say, "To find an article, use the index."

Use specific examples to make your point. Again, this is particularly true with instructional materials. Don't say, "If you want to find information on a topic, then type the 'Find' command followed by terms that describe the topic. Then hit the 'Enter' key." Instead say, "If you want to find information on cobras, type 'Find Su Cobras <Enter>'."

Be consistent in your use of terminology. Don't say, "Books are listed in the *online catalog*. Government documents are classified by a different system, but are included in the *electronic system* as well." Instead say, "Books are listed in the *online catalog*. Government documents are classified by a different system, but are included in the *online catalog* as well."

If listing items, make sure that the construction is parallel. Don't say, "There you can find books, journals, and published reports from government agencies." Instead say, "There you can find books, journals, and government documents."

Above all, stick to the facts, the information most useful to your users. Don't go off on tangents that are of more interest to you and other librarians than to your users. The information you include should cohere, held together by sentences and paragraphs. In general, each sentence you construct should begin with what is already known and lead to new knowledge at the end, e.g., "Once you've searched the database, hit <Enter> to see the list of articles." Sentences should be easily understood on first reading.

Paragraphs also follow the known-to-the-new progression. In a point-of-use guide, paragraphs are structured in relation to the instructional steps. Step 1 is one paragraph, step 2 is a second, and so on. There may be some exceptions to this, but you are writing a brief, step-by-step guide to a resource, not an exposition on its merits. Any elegance achieved by your writing style in a point-of-use guide will be through its simplicity.

EDITING

Editing a bibliography consists primarily of proofreading and copyediting. You may need to change your scheme for the organization of citations in order to make them more useful to your users, but the lack of narrative text (aside from an introduction or sometimes annotations) means you are checking primarily for mistakes of spelling and punctuation. Of course, you need to check for such errors in point-of-use materials too. Mistakes of usage and syntax are additional copyediting functions, and you need to ensure that your writing adheres to conventional standards in these areas. How you and your institution view those standards may vary, because the countless rules of grammar are of varying value. You will certainly want to make sure that your nouns and verbs agree ("you knowed that"). Whether you are concerned by finer points like split infinitives or the use of "that" for restrictive clauses may be a local matter. Remember that the main function of proper grammar is to make language easily understood. Minor deviations of fine points are sometimes tolerated, but clear-cut blunders are not. Keep a style manual handy.

Of more interest here is that you need to review point-of-use materials, whether drafted by you or someone else, with an editor's eye. You need to be prepared to delete, reorder, and revise—yes, change can be good. Do the instructions proceed in a logical order? Can they be followed in sequence without having to refer back to a previous step or prior section? If not, reorganize your text so that logic reigns supreme. If there are a few useful but parenthetical points you wish to make, it might be best to place these in their own section at the end of the guide as "helpful hints." Have an inexperienced user test the instructions for clarity and accuracy.

Is each instruction precisely written? Instructions can be confusing for many different reasons. You may be using words that are too complex or jargony. You may be using too many unnecessary words. Wordiness is a pernicious problem with instructions, and space is a major concern in a library guide. Pare ruthlessly. "Should this be the case" means "if." "Conduct a search" means "Search."

By contrast, don't use too few words to try to convey a complicated point. This problem sometimes surfaces when writers turn everything into nouns and modifiers and eliminate all articles and prepositions. It is good to delete unnecessary articles and prepositions, but not necessary ones. "Field-specific search strategy options are available" is fairly incomprehensible. "Another option is to search for terms that appear only in certain fields, like the author or title fields" is longer but much more readily understood. Saving space is important, but comprehension is more important.

As noted above, active sentence construction is superior to passive, especially for instructions. Instructions need to be written so that they are most easily understood by the user. Don't give the point of emphasis first. The command "Hit <F4> if you want to see the list of articles your search has retrieved" is confusing for a user. "If you want to see the list of articles your search has retrieved, hit <F4>" is better because it presents the information to the user in the order that it best can be understood.

The usual suspects of bad writing can be rounded up when

editing as well. Misplaced words and phrases, dangling modifiers, and awkward sentence construction all contribute strongly to muddied writing. You need to make whatever changes are necessary to make the text straightforward and simple.

LAYOUT OPTIONS

Once the words are right, it's time to work on the layout. This guide is part of a series; it does not stand on its own. Its design and layout should be consistent with other guides produced by your library. If your library has a logo, you'll want to incorporate that into the nameplate for your series. The nameplate of your guide is not likely to be as fancy as that of a newsletter and should accomplish three things: (1) identify the name of the library producing it, (2) clearly and concisely define what the user will learn by reading the guide, and (3) provide a graphically appealing appearance to the guide.

The layout for the body of the guide is made up of typographical, spatial, and, sometimes, graphic elements. While page-layout software can be very useful in working with these elements, word processing software can effectively handle them as well. The layout for a bibliography will rely primarily on typography and space to make the bibliographic citations easy to read and easy to distinguish from one another. Make an effort to assure that these elements are used consistently, both in this particular guide and in the series as a whole.

A number of typographic elements can help in this way (see Figure 9.1). You can use a mix of upper and lower cases or all capitals. You can use normal weight, or boldface, or italic type. You can use boldface, italic, or underlined type. You can use a variety of point sizes. You can use all of these effects, each indicating a different function.

Using spatial elements, you can arrange your page in many ways (see Figure 9.2). You can use indents, tabs, and block paragraphs. You can use graphic devices such as lines, boxes, and tinted screens to section off the page. You can break up the page by inserting blank lines between textual elements.

Point-of-use guides will use these same sorts of cues to format the page, but they do feature additional concerns. Your layout needs to provide the page with a flow that echoes the ordering sequence of the instructions. In other words, the reader needs to be able easily to find where to start on the page and where to go

---

FIGURE 9.1 Using Typographic Cues in a Bibliography

No Typographic Cues

Branch, Katherine, ed. Sourcebook for Bibliographic Instruction. Chicago, IL: Bibliographic Instruction Section, Association of College and Research Libraries, 1993.
Cubberley, Carol W. "Write Procedures that Work," in Library Journal, September 15, 1991, v116, 42-5.
Edsall, Marian S. Library Promotion Handbook. Phoenix, AZ: Oryx Press, 1980.
Hartley, James. Designing Instructional Text. London: Kogan Page, 1978.

Bold Name
Underlined Title

Branch, Katherine, ed. <u>Sourcebook for Bibliographic Instruction</u>. Chicago, IL: Bibliographic Instruction Section, Association of College and Research Libraries, 1993.
Cubberley, Carol W. "Write Procedures that Work," in <u>Library Journal</u>, September 15, 1991, v116, 42-5.
Edsall, Marian S. <u>Library Promotion Handbook</u>. Phoenix, AZ: Oryx Press, 1980.
Hartley, James. <u>Designing Instructional Text</u>. London: Kogan Page, 1978.

All Caps Name
Underlined Title

BRANCH, KATHERINE, ed. <u>Sourcebook for Bibliographic Instruction</u>. Chicago, IL: Bibliographic Instruction Section, Association of College and Research Libraries, 1993.
CUBBERLEY, CAROL W. "Write Procedures that Work," in <u>Library Journal</u>, September 15, 1991, v116, 42-5.
EDSALL, MARIAN S. <u>Library Promotion Handbook</u>. Phoenix, AZ: Oryx Press, 1980.
HARTLEY, JAMES. <u>Designing Instructional Text</u>. London: Kogan Page, 1978.

Bold Name
Italic Title

Branch, Katherine, ed. *Sourcebook for Bibliographic Instruction*. Chicago, IL: Bibliographic Instruction Section, Association of College and Research Libraries, 1993.
Cubberley, Carol W. "Write Procedures that Work," in *Library Journal*, September 15, 1991, v116, 42-5.
Edsall, Marian S. *Library Promotion Handbook*. Phoenix, AZ: Oryx Press, 1980.
Hartley, James. *Designing Instructional Text*. London: Kogan Page, 1978.

FIGURE 9.2 Using Spatial Cues in a Bibliography

No Typographic Cues
Interline Spacing

Branch, Katherine, ed. Sourcebook
for Bibliographic Instruction.
Chicago, IL: Bibliographic Instruction Section, Association of College and Research Libraries, 1993.

Cubberley, Carol W. "Write Procedures that Work," in Library Journal, September 15, 1991, v116, 42-
5.

Edsall, Marian S. Library Promotion Handbook. Phoenix, AZ: Oryx
Press, 1980.

Hartley, James. Designing Instructional Text. London: Kogan Page,
1978.

No Typographic Cues
Each Element Begins New Line
Interline Spacing

Branch, Katherine, ed.
Sourcebook for Bibliographic Instruction.
Chicago, IL: Bibliographic Instruction Section, Association of College and Research Libraries, 1993.

Cubberley, Carol W.
"Write Procedures that Work,"
in Library Journal,
September 15, 1991, v116, 42-5.

Edsall, Marian S.
Library Promotion Handbook.
Phoenix, AZ: Oryx Press, 1980.

Hartley, James.
Designing Instructional Text.
London: Kogan Page, 1978.

Typographic Cues
Interline Spacing

Branch, Katherine, ed. *Sourcebook*
for Bibliographic Instruction.
Chicago, IL: Bibliographic Instruction Section, Association of College and Research Libraries, 1993.

Cubberley, Carol W. "Write Procedures that Work," in *Library Jour-*
nal, September 15, 1991, v116, 42-
5.

Edsall, Marian S. *Library Promo-*
tion Handbook. Phoenix, AZ: Oryx
Press, 1980.

Hartley, James. *Designing Instruc-*
tional Text. London: Kogan Page,
1978.

Typographic Cues
Hanging Indent for Each Entry

Branch, Katherine, ed. *Sourcebook*
  for Bibliographic Instruction
  Chicago, IL: Bibliographic
  Instruction Section,
  Association of College and
  Research Libraries, 1993.
Cubberley, Carol W. "Write
  Procedures that Work," in
  Library Journal, September 15,
  1991, v116, 42-5.
Edsall, Marian S. *Library*
  Promotion Handbook. Phoenix,
  AZ: Oryx Press, 1980.
Hartley, James. *Designing*
  Instructional Text. London:
  Kogan Page, 1978.

next. The most obvious way to do so is by using numbered steps (see Figure 9.3).

However, with the effective use of spatial cues and typography, you can forego numbers if they do not seem appropriate to the guide. Spatial cues and typography can provide the requisite focal points of emphasis to make an attractive guide. Some point-of-use guides might be arranged better in a tabular format (see Figure 9.4). In addition, point-of-use materials can use graphic elements. Screen captures of the computer system being described can break up the page nicely and orient the user to the resource. Depending on the compatibility of your utility program for screen captures and your word processor or page-layout program, these can be easily imported into your guide.

TESTING

Once the editing and layout are complete (or so you hope), it's time to test the quality of your guide on some willing guinea pigs. It's a good idea to have more than one person try out your guide so you can get a number of different perspectives on its quality. Testing the text can be conducted before you lay out your design, but the two elements work in conjunction so it is best to test them that way.

Most libraries have a host of available guinea pigs to test guides. Support staff and student workers are prime candidates for this duty. Choose people who have a good eye for detail. They don't have to have any awareness of or interest in the subject of the guide in order to properly test its effectiveness. In a way, it's better if they are ignorant on the topic, for you will know that your guide truly works if they can fulfill the learning objectives of the text.

The most likely scenario is that your testers will give you feedback on what they understood and what they didn't. From that feedback, you'll make your revisions. The three main types of problems that might occur are strategic, structural, or tactical. Strategic errors are errors in planning. You may be trying to make one guide cover information that should be divided into two guides. Structural errors are errors of organization. Maybe you forgot a step or maybe you've arranged a bibliography in a manner that users can't make any sense of. Tactical errors are errors of writing. Your sentences may be confusing, your terminology inconsistent, or your grammar problematic. It's best if you let your

FIGURE 9.3 Numeric Ordering of a Point-of-Use Guide

GUIDE TO BASIC FUNCTIONS OF CUTCP SOFTWARE

I.   *Logging on to your account*
1)   Choose **Ethernet** from menu or as Windows icon
2)   Hold down **ALT** key and hit **A**
3)   At *Telnet>* prompt, enter appropriate machine name, i.e., pisces, cancer, clam...

II.   *TELNET to a non-Rutgers site*
1)   Choose **Ethernet** from menu or as Windows icon
2)   Hold down **ALT** key and hit **A**
3)   At *Telnet>* prompt, enter nominal or numeric address of site
4)   Follow appropriate logon procedures

III.   *Anonymous FTP*
1)   Choose **FTP** from menu or as Windows icon
2)   At *FTP>* prompt type **OPEN** followed by the nominal or numeric address of the FTP site
3)   Follow usual anonymous FTP procedures

IV.   *Transfer file from PC to Vax or Unix account (UPLOADING)*
1)   Follow steps 1-3 in section I above to log on to your account
2)   Get to the Vax (*$*) prompt
3)   Hold down the **ALT** key and hit **T** to FTP your PC
4)   Hold down the **ALT** key and hit **W** to transmit your logon password
5)   Standard FTP commands now apply. If you do a **DIR**, you will see a list of the files in the default directory (\cutcp\data)   on your PC.
6)   To upload a file from your PC to your computer account, type **GET** followed by the name of the file. A path can be specified if the file is not in the active directory. If multiple files with similar names need to be uploaded, you may use the **MGET** command and truncate the filename with the *.
7)   The system will prompt *TO LOCAL FILE:*. You can rename the file or simply hit <ENTER> to accept the existing filename.
8)   If the file is not an ASCII text file, type **BINARY** at the *FTP >* prompt before step 6.
9)   To exit, type **QUIT**.

FIGURE 9.4 Tabular Ordering of a Point-of-Use Guide

CD-ROM QUICK REFERENCE

FUNCTIONS	SILVERPLATTER	UMI	WILSON
FUNCTION KEYS			
F1	Help	Help	Help
F2	Find (Search)	Commands	Quit
F3	Database Guides	New Search	Change Disks
F4	Show (Display)	Output (Print)	Print This Record
F5	Index		Go to Citation
F6	Print	Word Index	Print/Download All Records
F7	Restart System	Skip Title List/ Display Abstracts	
F8	Change Disks	Order Form	
F9	Previous Record	Mark to Print	NA in Wilsearch
F10	Next Record	Restart System	NA in Wilsearch
GENERAL			
Help	F1	F1	F1
Change Disks	F8	ALTERNATE and F10	F3 (twice)
	Open CD Drawer	Open CD Drawer	Open CD Drawer
Quit	ESCAPE	F10	F2 or
	Q	Y	ESCAPE
		Choose *Exit*	
RETRIEVING			
Search	F2	F3	Select *New Search*
	Enter Terms	Enter Terms	Enter Terms
	RETURN	RETURN	END
			RETURN
Author Search	Lastname-Firstname in AU	AU(Lastname, Firstname)	On *Author/Name* Line:
			Lastname, Firstname or
			Firstname Lastname
Field Search	Search Term in Field Name	Field Name(Search Term)	Enter Terms on Proper Line of
			Input Screen
Truncate	*	?	: (end of word)
			# (within word)
Stop Search	CONTROL and BREAK	ESCAPE	ESCAPE
VIEWING			
Display	F4	RETURN or F7	RETURN
	RETURN		
Next Screen	F10 or PgDn	PgDn or +	RETURN
Previous Screen	F9 or PgUp	PgUp or -	F5
TRANSFERRING			
Print	F6	F4	F4 (this record) or
	TAB	RETURN (to print marked items)	F6 (all records)
	Indicate Record Numbers		
Download	ESCAPE	F4	F6
	T	Select *Output to Disk*	P
	Indicate Record Numbers	RETURN	A: Filename

testers check out your revised version of the guide to see if you've fixed the problem or created a new one.

Once completed, library guides need to be maintained and evaluated regularly. Nothing stays the same. New materials become available and need to be added to your bibliography. Or the focus of the bibliography's users changes over time and the bibliography needs to be altered to fit the new users' needs. Or the bibliography may have simply outlived its usefulness and needs to be retired.

Similarly, a point-of-use guide also needs to be updated. Indexes and computers systems change (especially the latter). Your guide needs to reflect those changes or it loses its effectiveness and is regarded suspiciously. System changes can be so minor that your guide needs to be only slightly revised. Or the changes could constitute a major system upgrade and warrant a complete rewrite of your guide. Don't neglect this step if you want your guides to be used.

Checklist for Library Guides

- Is the tone of the writing suitable to the material and audience? Is the language appropriate to the audience? Is there too much technical terminology or jargon? Are there too many words? Are terms used consistently? Are sentences well-constructed?
- Is the text clear and concise? Are instructions easily understood and properly ordered? Is the information correct? Is there enough information so that the user will be able to perform all major functions? Is there too much information so that the user has difficulty finding out how to do the two or three things he or she wants to do? Are headlines concise and descriptive?
- Is the point size of the type large enough? Is the mix of typefaces and styles done effectively? Are type styles used functionally and consistently?
- Is there enough white space on the page, or is there too much text crammed on the page? Is spacing used functionally to indicate new concepts? Is spacing used consistently?
- Is the nameplate attractive and identifiable? If there are screen captures or other illustrations, are they positioned on the page adjacent to the related text? Do the graphic elements open up the appearance of the page or constrict it?
- Have you signed and dated the guide so it can be easily evaluated and updated?

CAN THIS GUIDE BE SAVED?

Take a look at the guide in Figure 9.5. What can be done to improve it? Its main problem is that there is too much text crammed on the page. The guide needs white space to make it readable. Adding spacing between different sections of text and changing from justified alignment to ragged right can make a big difference. The text will need to be edited or it will need to extend onto additional pages, but it is more usable when it is more readable (see Figure 9.6).

The nameplate could also use some work. It is so small that it is barely noticeable. The type can be enlarged and rearranged, as in Figure 9.7. Finally, a smattering of graphic accents like tinted screens and rules can help orient the reader to the page's points of emphasis and improve the overall appearance of the page as well (see Figure 9.8).

PUBLISHING THE GUIDE

Just like a newsletter, library guides need to be reproduced in large quantities. The usual solution is the most cost-effective one: photocopying. The quality of a good photocopier is more than sufficient to reproduce an attractive library guide as long as you are copying from laser-printed originals. It is probable that your institution has an in-house copying operation or an outside copier of choice. If not, there are many to choose from, and costs are generally going to be pennies per page.

Guides are usually distributed as handouts. They may be given out at a library workshop or bibliographic instruction session. They almost certainly will be displayed in a prominent place in the library so that any user in need can freely take one. A new option is distribution via the World Wide Web. If your library has a Web site (see next chapter), then that is an ideal place to load the electronic versions of your library guides. Will they need to be revised to be loaded on the Web? Perhaps. If there are graphic elements or if they feature any tricks of layout, then some work will need to be done to fit them to the new format.

An easier way to preserve the page formatting is to transform the file into a .PDF document, where each page of the guide retains its original look but can't be edited. However, if they are

FIGURE 9.5 Can This Guide Be Saved?

ROBESON LIBRARY
RUTGERS CAMDEN
INFO GUIDE

USING PROQUEST UMI DATABASES

The Rutgers University Library System provides electronic access to UMI's Proquest family of databases via both CD-ROM technology and network connectivity. Computerized searching allows you to combine subject terms quickly and easily and gives you the ability to search many years at one time. **Available UMI databases include:**

PROQUEST DATABASE	CONTENT	YEARS
ABI/Inform	indexes 800 business journals	1988-date
Periodical Abstracts	indexes 1,600 magazines and journals on all topics	1986-date
Newspaper Abstracts	indexes the NYTimes, Wall Street Journal and other leading papers	1985-date

FORM A SEARCH STRATEGY

1. Choose search terms which best describe your topic. (One way to find related terms is to use the thesaurus for your database.)
2. Form a search strategy by combining your terms as described below.
   Use **AND** to find records which contain both term A and term B. This narrows the search.
   TARIFF AND IMPORT (will find citations which include both "tariff" and "import.")
   Use **OR** to find records which contain either term A or term B. This broadens the search.
   TARIFF OR TAX (will find citations which include either "tariff" or "tax.")

NETWORK ACCESS

Network access to these indexes is provided through the RLIN connection on INFO, the Rutgers Campus-Wide Information System. The databases are only available to those with Rutgers computer accounts. Searching aids and help can be found at the Reference desk.

SEARCH THE DATABASE

1. Type **INFO** at the system prompt for your RUNet account. Go into the Library submenus and select RLIN.
2. When connected to RLIN, type "1" for Bibliographic Files. The UMI files are called **ABI** (ABI/Inform), **PRA** (Periodical Abstracts) and **NRA** (Newspaper Abstracts.) Next, select the file or database you want by typing **SEL FIL {filename}.**
3. RLIN arranges its databases into searchable indexes. The main ones are: TW -- Title Word allows searches of words appearing in article titles; SW -- Subject Word allows searching for words appearing in; PN -- Personal Name allows for searching of authors, last name first.
4. Begin all searches with the FINd command, followed by index name and search terms, i.e., **FIN SW TELEVISION ADVERTISING**
5. To repeat a search in a different file, **SEL FIL {FILENAME}.** Then type **RES** for Resume.

VIEW THE RESULTS

1. For most searches, RLIN provides a MULtiple display (brief bibliographic citations) or a prompt (:MUL?) for the MULtiple display.
2. To page through these brief records, hit RETURN or ENTER.
3. To see the full record, type **LON {record number}**; to return to brief records, type **MUL {record number}.**

HELPFUL HINTS

1. To print records to a local printer, the command is **TYPE {record number range} {LON or MUL}.** Download according to the screen capture facilities of your telecommunications software.
2. To exit the system, type **LOGOFF**; to quit INFO, keep hitting "Q".
3. To get online help, type **HELP.** For search assistance, call the Reference desk at Robeson.

CD-ROM ACCESS

SEARCH THE DATABASE

1. Choose from the on-screen menu which lists the available databases.
2. From the UMI Menu screen, choose **Search...** by pressing RETURN or ENTER.
3. At the "Search term(s)" prompt, type in your search terms and hit RETURN or ENTER. At any time you may press the **F3** key to return to the search prompt and enter new search terms.
4. The number of bibliographic records containing the terms you selected will be indicated on the screen.
5. To reexecute an prior search in a different database, hold down the ALT key and hit **F10.** Choose **Change** from the UMI menu. At the Proquest Database menu, select the new database. Use the arrow keys to reenter search terms and hit RETURN or ENTER.

FIGURE 9.6 Adding White Space and Changing Focus

ROBESON LIBRARY
RUTGERS CAMDEN
INFO GUIDE

USING PROQUEST UMI NETWORK DATABASES

The Rutgers University Library System provides electronic access to UMI's Proquest family of databases via both CD-ROM technology and network connectivity. Computerized searching allows you to combine subject terms quickly and easily and gives you the ability to search many years at one time. **Available UMI databases include:**

PROQUEST DATABASE	CONTENT	YEARS
ABI/Inform	indexes 800 business journals	1988-date
Periodical Abstracts	indexes 1,600 magazines and journals on all topics	1986-date
Newspaper Abstracts	indexes the NYTimes, Wall Street Journal and other leading papers	1985-date

FORM A SEARCH STRATEGY

1. Choose search terms which best describe your topic. (One way to find related terms is to use the thesaurus for your database.)
2. Form a search strategy by combining your terms as described below.

    Use **AND** to find records which contain both term A and term B. This narrows the search.
    TARIFF AND IMPORT (will find citations which include both "tariff" and "import.")

    Use **OR** to find records which contain either term A or term B. This broadens the search.
    TARIFF OR TAX (will find citations which include either "tariff" or "tax.")

SEARCH THE DATABASE

1. Type **INFO** at the system prompt for your RUNet account. Go into the Library submenus and select RLIN.
2. When connected to RLIN, type "1" for Bibliographic Files. The UMI files are called **ABI** (ABI/Inform), **PRA** (Periodical Abstracts) and **NRA** (Newspaper Abstracts.) Next, select the file or database you want by typing **SEL FIL {filename}**.
3. RLIN arranges its databases into searchable indexes. The main ones are: TW -- Title Word allows searches of words appearing in article titles; SW -- Subject Word allows searching for words appearing in that field; PN -- Personal Name allows for searching of authors, last name first.
4. Begin all searches with the FINd command, followed by index name and search terms, i.e., **FIN SW TELEVISION ADVERTISING**
5. To repeat a search in a different file, **SEL FIL {FILENAME}**. Then type **RES** for Resume.

VIEW THE RESULTS

1. For most searches, RLIN provides a MULtiple display (brief bibliographic citations) or a prompt (:MUL?) for the MULtiple display.
2. To page through these brief records, hit RETURN or ENTER.
3. To see the full record, type **LON {record number}**; to return to brief records, type **MUL {record number}**.

HELPFUL HINTS

1. To print records to a local printer, the command is **TYPE {record number range} {LON or MUL}**. Download according to the screen capture facilities of your telecommunications software.
2. To exit the system, type **LOGOFF**; to quit INFO, keep hitting "Q".
3. To get online help, type **HELP**. For search assistance, call the Reference desk at Robeson.

FIGURE 9.7 Nameplate Makeover

 RUTGERS
UNIVERSITY

Using Proquest UMI Network Databases

ROBESON
INFO GUIDE

The Rutgers University Library System provides electronic access to UMI's Proquest family of databases via both CD-ROM technology and network connectivity. Computerized searching allows you to combine subject terms quickly and easily and gives you the ability to search many years at one time. **Available UMI databases include:**

PROQUEST DATABASE	CONTENT	YEARS
ABI/Inform	indexes 800 business journals	1988-date
Periodical Abstracts	indexes 1,600 magazines and journals on all topics	1986-date
Newspaper Abstracts	indexes the NYTimes, Wall Street Journal and other leading papers	1985-date

FORM A SEARCH STRATEGY

1. Choose search terms which best describe your topic. (One way to find related terms is to use the thesaurus for your database.)
2. Form a search strategy by combining your terms as described below.

Use **AND** to find records which contain both term A and term B. This narrows the search.
TARIFF AND IMPORT (will find citations which include both "tariff" and "import.")

Use **OR** to find records which contain either term A or term B. This broadens the search.
TARIFF OR TAX (will find citations which include either "tariff" or "tax.")

SEARCH THE DATABASE

1. Type **INFO** at the system prompt for your RUNet account. Go into the Library submenus and select RLIN.
2. When connected to RLIN, type "1" for Bibliographic Files. The UMI files are called **ABI** (ABI/Inform), **PRA** (Periodical Abstracts) and **NRA** (Newspaper Abstracts.) Next, select the file or database you want by typing **SEL FIL {filename}.**
3. RLIN arranges its databases into searchable indexes. The main ones are: TW -- Title Word allows searches of words appearing in article titles; SW -- Subject Word allows searching for words appearing in that field; PN -- Personal Name allows for searching of authors, last name first.
4. Begin all searches with the FINd command, followed by index name and search terms, i.e., **FIN SW TELEVISION ADVERTISING**
5. To repeat a search in a different file, **SEL FIL {FILENAME}.** Then type **RES** for Resume.

VIEW THE RESULTS

1. For most searches, RLIN provides a MULtiple display (brief bibliographic citations) or a prompt (:MUL?) for the MULtiple display.
2. To page through these brief records, hit RETURN or ENTER.
3. To see the full record, type **LON {record number}**; to return to brief records, type **MUL {record number}.**

HELPFUL HINTS

1. To print records to a local printer, the command is **TYPE {record number range} {LON or MUL}.** Download according to the screen capture facilities of your telecommunications software.
2. To exit the system, type **LOGOFF**; to quit INFO, keep hitting "Q".
3. To get online help, type **HELP**. For search assistance, call the Reference desk at Robeson.

FIGURE 9.8 Adding Graphics

UTGERS
UNIVERSITY

Using Proquest UMI Network Databases

OBESON
INFO GUIDE

The Rutgers University Library System provides electronic access to UMI's Proquest family of databases via both CD-ROM technology and network connectivity. Computerized searching allows you to combine subject terms quickly and easily and gives you the ability to search many years at one time. **Available UMI databases include:**

PROQUEST DATABASE	CONTENT	YEARS
ABI/Inform	indexes 800 business journals	1988-date
Periodical Abstracts	indexes 1,600 magazines and journals on all topics	1986-date
Newspaper Abstracts	indexes the NYTimes, Wall Street Journal and other leading papers	1985-date

FORM A SEARCH STRATEGY

1. Choose search terms which best describe your topic. (One way to find related terms is to use the thesaurus for your database.)
2. Form a search strategy by combining your terms as described below.

   Use **AND** to find records which contain both term A and term B. This narrows the search.
   TARIFF AND IMPORT (will find citations which include both "tariff" and "import.")

   Use **OR** to find records which contain either term A or term B. This broadens the search.
   TARIFF OR TAX (will find citations which include either "tariff" or "tax.")

SEARCH THE DATABASE

1. Type **INFO** at the system prompt for your RUNet account. Go into the Library submenus and select RLIN.
2. When connected to RLIN, type "1" for Bibliographic Files. The UMI files are called **ABI** (ABI/Inform), **PRA** (Periodical Abstracts) and **NRA** (Newspaper Abstracts.) Next, select the file or database you want by typing **SEL FIL {filename}.**
3. RLIN arranges its databases into searchable indexes. The main ones are: TW -- Title Word allows searches of words appearing in article titles; SW -- Subject Word allows searching for words appearing in that field; PN -- Personal Name allows for searching of authors, last name first.
4. Begin all searches with the FINd command, followed by index name and search terms, i.e., **FIN SW TELEVISION ADVERTISING**
5. To repeat a search in a different file, **SEL FIL {FILENAME}.** Then type **RES** for Resume.

VIEW THE RESULTS

1. For most searches, RLIN provides a MULtiple display (brief bibliographic citations) or a prompt (:MUL?) for the MULtiple display.
2. To page through these brief records, hit RETURN or ENTER.
3. To see the full record, type **LON {record number}**; to return to brief records, type **MUL {record number}.**

HELPFUL HINTS

1. To print records to a local printer, the command is **TYPE {record number range} {LON or MUL}.** Download according to the screen capture facilities of your telecommunications software.
2. To exit the system, type **LOGOFF**; to quit INFO, keep hitting "Q".
3. To get online help, type **HELP.** For search assistance, call the Reference desk at Robeson.

essentially ASCII text files, then they can be uploaded essentially as is. If you use the "Preformatted" HTML code (see chapter 11), you can maintain the guide's appearance with very little work on your part. Once loaded on the library server, the guide is available at any time of day to anyone able to access the library's Web site. This is particularly helpful for guides that outline how to use databases available via remote access.

On the WWW, library guides can be seen clearly as promotional instruments for library services to a very wide audience. Printed library guides are promotional instruments too. Using desktop publishing principles and tools, you can create well-designed guides that serve the best interests of your library and your users. Well-designed library guides make users aware of library services and resources and teach users how to use them.

SECTION 4
WORLD WIDE WEB PAGES

10 ELECTRONIC BLUEPRINTS: PLANNING A WORLD WIDE WEB HOME PAGE

"You're traveling through another dimension. A dimension not only of sight and sound, but of mind. A wondrous land whose boundaries are that of imagination," Rod Serling would intone at the beginning of each episode of the television science fiction program *The Twilight Zone*. The World Wide Web (WWW) is such a dimension for desktop publishing, primarily because a page on the WWW is alive. There is no "putting it to bed," as the old newspaper expression goes, meaning to print and publish the issue with finality. The Web is too much in flux to truly compare a page with a static printed page.

The digital page is alive in at least three ways. First, it is always "under construction." You can never say, "I'm all done," because several of those links you've provided on that page have changed or moved or simply vanished, and new sites of interest that you want to add have come online. You must do as the Red Queen in *Through the Looking Glass* did, and run twice as fast to stay in the same place.

Second, your server may change. You may need to change the site of your page, i.e., the computer or the directory structure of the computer. The text and graphics of a printed newsletter do not migrate to another ream of paper once the newsletter has been published; traditional publication provides permanence to the printed page. Not so the Web.

Third, to quote *The Outer Limits*, another science fiction television program from the 1960s, "There is nothing wrong with your television set. Do not attempt to adjust the picture. We are controlling transmission. We will control the horizontal; we will control the vertical . . . " In short, desktop publishers on the Web lose a great deal of control over how their pages will look. Much of the typography and layout are controlled by the Web browser being employed by the user to navigate the Web. You may design your page so that it is laid out just as you like, but someone looking at your page may have set the "Preferences" option of their browsing software so that it uses completely different typefaces and styles from the ones you have chosen. And for those who find your page using a graphical browser that is different from yours, the layout itself may look entirely different. Those using text-based browsers like Lynx will receive an even more disparate view of your page.

A LITTLE BACKGROUND

So what is the Web and what are its advantages, you may wonder. The World Wide Web was created by CERN, a high-energy physics laboratory in Switzerland, to link information on the Internet in a manner that models the way people think, that is, in an interconnected but nonlinear fashion. The Web creates a global information system from the merger of the techniques of Hypertext and information retrieval. Access to the WWW is primarily provided by any number of browsers or user-friendly interfaces to the WWW. Graphical browsers run in the Macintosh, Windows, or X Windows (a windowing system for Unix-based network machines) environments and provide access to multimedia resources containing text, images, sound, and animation— all of which can be viewed or played on your personal computer. Connections are embedded in each document as Hypertext links, usually notated by underlined words or graphics, that you point to and click on to retrieve a file or visit a site electronically. Netscape, Mosaic, Cello, and Lynx are some of the browsers available. [Lynx provides access to the WWW without the multimedia display for those who only can muster VT100 terminal emulation or who are connected to the Internet via a modem with a baud rate under 14.4.]

Hypertext links are based on the URL or Uniform Resource Locator, which is the system of network addressing used on the World Wide Web. A URL consists of a scheme (the type of resource), the network address, path, and filename; the use pattern is scheme://host.domain/path/file.ext. For example, http://www.whitehouse.gov is the URL for the White House's home page. The scheme "HTTP" stands for Hypertext Transport Protocol, which is a standard type of site on the WWW. The scheme might also be "file" or "telnet" or "gopher" or "wais" or "news."

Sites on the World Wide Web are referred to as pages or home pages, with home pages referring to top level pages. Web pages are constructed using HTML, the Hypertext Markup Language. HTML permits you to embed direct point-and-click links to other sites or URLs within your own document. HTML allows you to designate on-screen formatting and utilize URLs to point to other

A Brief Glossary of Web-Related Terms

Browser—a user-friendly interface that provides access to the WWW. Graphical browsers, like Netscape or Mosaic, allow a user to point-and-click with a mouse to navigate the web. Text-based browsers like Lynx offer access to the WWW to users with text-based terminals.

Clickable—the ability to point and click on underlined words or graphics to retrieve the indicated file.

FTP—File Transfer Protocol, i.e., the mechanism for transferring files between two remote computers.

GIF—Graphic Interchange Format was developed by Compuserv and is used as a format for images on the WWW.

Gopher—software that provides menu-driven access to resources on the Internet. Documents are arranged hierarchically in a series of menus. Menu choices might be actual files, access points for telnet sites, or simply tunnels to other gophers.

Home Page—the top level or main menu page at a WWW site. It provides links to subordinate pages at that site.

HTML—HyperText Markup Language in which Web pages are written. HTML permits one to embed direct point-and-click links to other sites or URLs within the display of your document.

HTTP—HyperText Transport Protocol which is the standard type of site on the WWW, the hypertext web page.

Hypertext—text that includes jump points or links to related files or documents.

The Internet—a collection of connections; it is the interconnection of thousands of institutional, state, regional, and national computer networks that forms a worldwide matrix of information connectivity.

JPEG—the Joint Photographic Experts Group format for images found on the WWW.

Link—connection to a related file or document.

Listservs, listservers, or lists—computer conferences to which a user subscribes. Postings to the list are received as electronic mail messages.

Tags—coding for text markup language like HTML. These codes define how a page will display on screen and link to other pages. Tags themselves do not display on screen.

Telnet—facility for remote log-in, i.e., the ability to connect to a computer at a remote location and to access that computer as if the user were locally connected to it.

Unix—operating system prevalent on the Internet and WWW.

URL—Uniform Resource Locator which is the system of network addressing used on the World Wide Web.

Usenet—a UNIX-based electronic bulletin board network which provides access to well over 1,000 news groups or computer conferences.

WAIS—the Wide Area Information Server is an information retrieval system that can perform full-text Boolean searches on a variety of sources.

World Wide Web, WWW, or W3—created by CERN, a high energy physics laboratory in Switzerland, to link information on the Internet in an interconnected, nonlinear fashion. The Web creates a global information system from the merger of the techniques of hypertext and information retrieval.

resources, which may be other Web pages, gophers, ftp archives, and so on. The HTML programming codes do not display on the screen, but can be viewed on command.

Figure 10.1 demonstrates what a WWW page looks like when viewed using Netscape; Figure 10.2 shows the HTML coding used to create the screen.

An alternative to HTML is Java, which may be the next big development on the Web. A page written in Java and accessed by a Java browser like Hot Java enables the user to load images, sound and animation files, spreadsheets, and more on a PC without having first loaded the appropriate software (e.g., viewers or players), on that machine. The Java link takes care of all software considerations, in effect becoming the operating system for the local machine. While there are some Java sites now available, it is still an up-and-coming technology, at least 30 nanoseconds away. So for now, we are concerned with HTML.

You must learn the HTML programming codes in order to "publish" a page on the Web, and those codes will be discussed in chapter 11. In terms of desktop publishing, pages can be designed and coded using an HTML editing program, and these vary in the amount of menu-driven handholding they provide. An easier choice for most people is to use the existing word processor to enter the text, and then add the HTML coding to the word processor file. You would then save the file as an ASCII file so it could be uploaded to your server. The coding can be done manually or, with many of the better word processors like WordPerfect, by using an HTML plug-in to the word processor. A plug-in allows you to add extensive coding with simple commands and saves you some keystrokes. In either case, you first need to understand the codes. Some page-layout programs like PageMaker have also come out with HTML add-ons to their ba-

---

FIGURE 10.1 WWW Page Viewed on a Netscape Browser

Librarians at the Paul Robeson Library

There are seven full time librarians at the Paul Robeson Library on the Camden campus of Rutgers University.

- ☐ Gary Golden, Director
- ☐ Susan Beck
- ☐ Jean Crescenzi
- ☐ Theo Haynes
- ☐ John Maxymuk
- ☐ Jim Nettleman
- ☐ Julie Still

 Return to Robeson Home Page

E-mail any questions or comments to:
maxymuk@crab.rutgers.edu
http://www.rutgers.edu/rulib/camden/libn.htm
Updated 12/25/95

---

sic software. We are now seeing the advent of graphical HTML authoring software such as Microsoft FrontPage which allows you to view the page's appearance as you create it and to avoid having to key in coding.

BASIC PLANNING QUESTIONS

Once you've learned the codes and decided on what software you will use to design your pages, you are faced with some familiar questions. Who is your audience, and what is your message? What do you want to offer to the world? There is a wide variety of

---

FIGURE 10.2 HTML Coding for Figure 10.1

```
<TITLE>Librarians at the Paul Robeson Library</TITLE>

<center> <img src="/cloudclh.gif" alt""> </center>
<head>
<H1> <b>Librarians at the Paul Robeson Library</b> </H1> </head>
<p>
<body>
There are seven full time librarians at the Paul Robeson Library
on the Camden campus of Rutgers University.

<UL>
<li><A HREF="golden.html">Gary Golden, Director</A>
<li><A HREF="beck.html">Susan Beck</A>
<li><A HREF="crescenz.html">Jean Crescenzi</A>
<li><A HREF="haynes.html">Theo Haynes</A>
<li><A HREF="maxymuk.htm">John Maxymuk</A>
<li><A HREF="nettlem.html">Jim Nettleman</A>
<li><A HREF="still.html">Julie Still</A>
</UL>
<p>
<A HREF="robe.html"><img src="/back.gif" alt=""<strong> Return to
Robeson Home Page
</strong> </a> <p>
E-mail any questions or comments to:</body>

<address> maxymuk@crab.rutgers.edu <br>
http://www.rutgers.edu/rulib/camden/libn.htm <br>
Updated 12/25/95 </address>
```

---

both trivial and essential information published on the Web. For example, I verified the accuracy of the two quotations that opened this chapter by consulting sites on the WWW. *The Twilight Zone* opening is reprinted as text (http://home.ptd.net/~jseward/); *The Outer Limits* beginning is recorded as an audio file that can be played back (http://www.webzone1.co.uk/www/brendan/ outer.htm).

As a librarian, there are a number of different types of pages you may be planning. You may be designing an overall set of pages for your institution, a page devoted to online resources on a particular subject, a personal page on you as a professional, or even a personal page on your after-hours interests. If you are working on a set of pages for an institution, then you may very well be working on all of these page varieties and developing a structure to link them all logically.

Your potential audience is effectively the entire world, but you will be aiming at a smaller subset of that. Just because the entire world can barge through your electronic doorway doesn't mean you need to provide toys to make everyone happy. There may be some services or features you want to make broadly available, and some whose access you want to limit to a select audience. For example, an academic institution may provide a gateway service to federal government WWW sites open to anyone with Internet access. At the same time, that institution may limit access to students, staff, and faculty for other resources, such as indexes, for which the institution pays a subscription fee.

Another factor you must determine about your target audience is what software they will use to access this page. As indicated above, the user's browser has an enormous impact on how the page will appear. In designing your page, take into account that one-third of your users may be viewing your page via Lynx, another third via Netscape, and the final third from a variety of graphical browsers (see Figures 10.3 and 10.4).

Such a breakdown might affect your HTML coding in a number of ways. You may want to include text alternatives to graphics, particularly graphics that are clickable links, so that your Lynx users are greeted with a pleasant and usable display. You may want to avoid creating pages that rely on the user's browser being set to a certain page width or being able to support particular colors. You may also choose to incorporate more logical mark-up tags like those that indicate if type should be "strong" or "emphatic," rather than physical mark-up tags like those for boldface or italics. Logical tags are more likely to be consistently applied by all browsers.

While these issues are unique to the digital world, the most important item for any type of page, printed or electronic, is still the message. What information are you trying to convey? Are you trying to make library policies and procedures more available? Describe the scope of the collection and the mission of the library? Provide maps and/or photographs of the library? Include personal pages for individual librarians outlining their backgrounds, responsibilities, and interests? Is this a way to disseminate library handouts and guides more broadly? Are you creating pages for specific events or groups (such as academic courses)? Establishing a presence on the Internet for your library? Making the library catalog and indexes as well as any in-house databases widely accessible? Providing a gateway to subject resources on the WWW? All of the above?

Because of the variety of focuses, it is a good idea for your library to draft a set of policy and content guidelines for two reasons. First, so everyone will understand the purpose of the pages

FIGURE 10.3 WWW Page from Figure 10.1 Viewed via Mosaic

Librarians at the Paul Robeson Library

There are seven full time librarians at the Paul Robeson
Library on the Camden campus of Rutgers University.

    Gary Golden, Director
    Susan Beck
    Jean Crescenzi
    Theo Haynes
    John Maxymuk
    Jim Nettleman
    Julie Still

 Return to Robeson Home Page

E-mail any questions or comments to:

maxymuk@crab.rutgers.edu
http://www.rutgers.edu/rulib/camden/libn.htm
Updated 12/25/95

FIGURE 10.4 WWW Page from Figure 10.1 Viewed via Lynx

                    Librarians at the Paul Robeson Library (p1 of 2)

    [IMAGE]

                    LIBRARIANS AT THE PAUL ROBESON LIBRARY

    There are seven full time librarians at the Paul Robeson Library on
    the Camden campus of Rutgers University.
       * [1]Gary Golden, Director
       * [2]Susan Beck
       * [3]Jean Crescenzi
       * [4]Theo Haynes
       * [5]John Maxymuk
       * [6]Jim Nettleman
       * [7]Julie Still

    [8]Return to Robeson Home Page
    -- press space for next page --
     Arrow keys: Up and Down to move. Right to follow a link; Left to go back.
    H)elp O)ptions P)rint G)o M)ain screen Q)uit /=search [delete]=history list
    ± pisces   12 36

                    Librarians at the Paul Robeson Library (p2 of 2)

    E-mail any questions or comments to:
    maxymuk@crab.rutgers.edu
    http://www.rutgers.edu/rulib/camden/libn.htm
    Updated 12/25/95

    Commands: Use arrow keys to move, '?' for help, 'q' to quit, '<-' to go back
     Arrow keys: Up and Down to move. Right to follow a link; Left to go back.
    H)elp O)ptions P)rint G)o M)ain screen Q)uit /=search [delete]=history list
    ± pisces   12:36

and what they aim to accomplish. Second, so anyone designing a page will have a framework from which to work.

ORGANIZATION

Guidelines can specify fine details such as where and how to sign your page or the proper use of official logos. Of more importance, the guidelines should stipulate what type of information is to be included and how it is to be organized. The need for organization is common to all publications, but the WWW offers unique challenges and opportunities. On the Web, the structure is nonlinear, and multiple-access points are not only possible but desirable. The key is to provide an organizing structure and to give that structure balance so that there are neither too few or too many layers of pages.

If your home page is one very long menu that provides direct access to every link on every page, then the result is overwhelming and frustrating to the user. Conversely, if your home page leads to menus that lead to menus that lead to menus that lead to menus that finally lead to some pages with actual content, then you've designed a hierarchical gopher, not a Web site, and you are not taking full advantage of the linking capabilities of the Web. Somewhere in between these two extremes you will find the right balance for your mix of content and connections. Just as when you plan an addition to the book stacks, you need to allow for growth in your overall structure. Your pages and their connections will only expand as more and more information migrates to the WWW.

As a page grows, it will need to be redesigned and probably broken up into multiple pages when it gets too unwieldy. "How large is too large?" is yet another question for your institution to grapple with. You may choose to limit the number of links any one page may contain. Or your limit could be based on the byte size of the page; lengthy pages take longer to load, and lengthy pages with graphics take even longer. Or you may simply let the classification of the page's subject matter be the deciding factor. Content should be of highest importance. Again, it is a matter of balance. Accessing a large number of very short pages can take longer and be more frustrating to a user than a few fairly large pages. Maintaining a large number of short pages can be more of a challenge for the Web author(s) trying to keep all of that disparate information in a coherent structure. On the other hand, scrolling through pages of more than two or three screens can be difficult and disorienting.

FROM THE TOP DOWN

No matter how many pages there are or how large each is, there will be a single, top-level, home page, which will set the tone and define the structure of the entire Web site. From the top-level home page on down, a Web site can be organized in a number of ways.

Your top-level page may feature a clickable image map that provides connections to second-level menu pages. The image map may be a floorplan of the library, an illustration that graphically and clearly delineates the organizing structure of the site, or a console of labeled buttons. Image maps are very impressive looking, but are moderately complicated to master, take longer to load, and cannot be viewed by text-based browsers. For text-based browsers, a text alternative would need to be included.

Another graphic approach to your top-level page is to use a brochure style that incorporates nonclickable images with text-based links to second-level menu pages. This type of page is heavy on the design side but can be very attractive to look at, although somewhat slow to load. Text-based browsers won't display the images, but the textual links make this approach viable in that environment.

Your top-level page can also be organized as a hierarchical menu with the menu structure based on institutional departments, services, functions, or on an overall subject orientation. This style is largely textual but may feature an occasional image such as a photograph of the institution or the library or the logo of either. Not as flashy as the more image-laden styles, a hierarchical menu is easily read by a text-based browser. It can also include more choices and a more extensive classification of information than can a more graphically oriented format. You may also choose some sort of combination of these types or come up with your own form.

The resulting structure is held together by the links contained on the pages. The content of the pages and links can help determine your structure. If you are putting up a tutorial or guided tour, you might use a sequential structure, which would connect page 1 to page 2 to page 3 with occasional prescribed variables (page 2 can go to page 2a or 2b). Each page would also offer the opportunity to jump back a page or jump back to the beginning.

If you are putting up an organizational chart or a subject classification of a collection, you might choose a more hierarchical structure. In this matrix-like setup of topics and levels, you can link to any pages on the same level or move up and down along a topic. However, you cannot move to a lower level on a different topic. In this matrix, you can travel by rows or columns, but not diagonally.

Or you could use a more free-form approach that permits the user more latitude in linking among your cluster of pages. It's a good idea to try to diagram the organizational structure of your pages before you start writing them, because that structure will have a strong effect on what you include. The diagram will be useful when you update or add pages to your site.

What you are aiming for is to create a structure that users can easily understand and navigate without difficulty. Think of the needs and thought processes of your users when classifying information. Try to include resources in the manner users will search for them—listing information by its format, for example, may not be the best arrangement. There should be a consistent look to all the pages at a site so that the user can gain familiarity in finding what he or she wants. But there should also be a distinctive look as well. The Web is a multimedia environment after all; logos, photographs, and typography are all at your disposal. Take advantage of what is offered, but don't forget the text-based user.

TECHNICAL ISSUES

It is a good idea for your site's address to be user friendly. An identifiable "domain name alias" masks the actual name of the machine where your files are located. The name of the machine where your files reside now may be hephzibah.rutgers.edu. If you use an alias so that the user sees your URL as http://www.rutgers.edu/home.html, then you realize two benefits: first, the name can be easily noted by the user; and second, the URL remains the same, even if your site moves to another machine, and the change is transparent to users.

The structure of your directories on the server should likewise be user friendly. Directory and file names should be brief, clear, and descriptive. Practical questions regarding where the files will reside, who will load them on the machine, who will maintain them, who will monitor the links, and how the whole mechanism will happen also need to be resolved within your institution. These sorts of technical issues may need to be handled by your computing gurus, and you will need to maintain good relations with the more technically inclined if you are not an expert in this area yourself.

NAVIGATION

How will a user get around within your site? How will a user get from your site to others you think he or she will want to visit? The answer to both questions is by using Hypertext links, the basis for the structure of the Web itself.

Within your site, the user may want to consult the catalog, indexes, in-house databases, maps, uploaded library guides, lists of online subject resources, or any mixture of the above. Beyond your site, the user may want to check out subject resources you have listed that will in turn lead to other pages not included in your links, or to use one of the many searchable indexes of WWW resources such as Yahoo in order to further explore the Web. Your institution may limit the links on your page to only those offering noncommercial services, those readily accessible, or those meeting certain evaluative, local criteria. All links need to be regularly checked to ensure that they are still active and useful. If not, they must be deleted and perhaps replaced by something new.

Much of what library sites do is provide menuing and subject guidance to the resources on the Web via these types of links. In addition to standard home pages, there are Hypertext documents on the Web, an example of which would be a scholarly paper in which you can click on a footnote number and call up the bibliographic citation or, better yet, the actual full text of the article cited. From a Hypertext document, you might also be able to click on a word and call up its definition or any items of interest the creator of the Hypertext document thought would provide greater depth to your understanding.

Navigating among all of these sorts of links requires one final type of connection, the "go to" link, which takes the user to other areas of the same site—perhaps a previous page, the next page, the next level up, an overall table of contents, or the top-level menu. In Figure 10.3, "Return to Robeson Home Page" is a "go to" link. All pages should include "go to" links so the user can feel some semblance of direction in this unfettered environment. By providing one or more of these links at the bottom and/or top of each page, you help keep the user from getting lost in your section of the Web.

PAGE DESIGN

Keeping the user from getting lost is one effect of good page design. Another effect is capturing the user's interest. The basic principles of good digital page design are similar to those for the printed page:

- The text should be clear and legible.
- The most important features or information should be given prominence and emphasis on the page or screen.
- White space should be ample enough so that the page or screen does not look cluttered.
- Graphics should be large enough to make out, but not so large or plentiful that they overwhelm the page or screen
- The mix of text, white space, and graphics should be balanced, consistent, and pleasing.

The challenge presented by Web pages is that you have limited control over elements of the layout in comparison to the control you have over the printed page. Besides, no matter how hard you work to achieve just the right layout, it will look different to users employing other browsers or who have set the options differently on their browsers. One example of this is the use of color in Web pages. Many pages on the Web feature color backgrounds, but the color you choose when designing the page is not necessarily the color users are seeing when viewing that page with their browsers. Color choices that look great in the original design may make a page unreadable for many users. Colored and graphic backgrounds should be used with extreme care because of the potential for illegible results. Ask people who use different browsers to critique the appearance of your page in their environment.

Space, white or otherwise, can be added in many ways and should be used to help to organize the page visually. Indenting is one way, and that works particularly well with lists of resources. Space between lines of text can be added with the line break or paragraph codes. The main thing in using blank lines between sections of text is to do so consistently. If you want to use a single blank line between paragraphs and two between sections, that's fine, but do it the same way every time. If you want to use an indent to indicate a paragraph and a single blank line to divide sections, that's fine too. Just be consistent.

Tricks can be employed to change the default margins or to supply blank space of essentially any dimension, but to start you may want to accept the default values and stick to basics. In the interests of consistency, you might want to create a template file to handle the basic layout issues.

Typographic tools are severely limited on the Web. Choosing a typeface and point size is meaningless, because the typeface and size the user will see is the one his or her browser is set to. What you are left with are some basic tools to indicate emphasis, like bold and strong; a handful of different formats for lists; and a series of heading levels to indicate relative type size. Heading levels are labeled one through six, with one the largest and six the smallest in relative point size. Netscape has added some enhancements such as a simple centering code and a primitive font-sizing code. These codes will not be understood by non-Netscape browsers, though. What this boils down to is don't get too cute. And please avoid the Netscape blinking text "enhancement." You have a handful of basic tools; use them judiciously and consistently, and your page may achieve a simple elegance. If you try to use all six levels of headings, use your spacing erratically, or overdo the use of emphatics, then your page will look like a jumbled mess.

Graphics are the final element in page design, and they come in two basic varieties, in-line or external. In-line graphics are images that load as part of your page right next to the text. External images (and other audiovisual files such as audio files and movie or animation files) must be selected from a link on your page and will then load separately. In-line images must be incorporated into your page design.

There are some rules of thumb when dealing with in-line images. Keep them small (under 20K), sparse (no more than two or three to a page), and tasteful (no comment). Graphics generally look better wide than tall. They fit better on screens, which are usually aligned to the left, and allow a better arrangement of text. One way to keep graphics small is to use "thumbnails" whenever possible. Thumbnails are reduced representations of external images. If the user clicks on the thumbnail, the full-sized external image is displayed on the screen. Using thumbnails will keep your page design simple and page-loading time short. Size them so that they will fully display within the screen of a standard 14" or 15" monitor. (Monitor displays are measured in pixels. Each pixel is a dot of light on the screen, and a 14" monitor measures roughly 640 wide x 480 high pixels.) This is particularly important for a banner graphic of the logo of your institution which you might be running at the top of each page; size it so that it doesn't run off the screen. All of these sizing functions as well as other graphics editing are accomplished using graphics software like Adobe Photoshop.

Graphics are generally either .GIF (Graphic Interchange Format) or .JPG (Joint Photographic Experts Group) files. Generally, GIFs are larger and take longer to load, but are better for line art. JPEGs use compression techniques and are ideally suited for photographs; comparable GIF files consist of considerably more bytes. GIF images can be either interlaced or noninterlaced. Interlaced GIFs are transmitted gradually. First, a low-resolution image is transmitted to the user. Then, the image is upgraded to a high-resolution one with each successive transfer of data. Noninterlaced images transmit the image's finished form a little at a time. Interlaced images take as long as noninterlaced ones to load fully. However, because the whole image is present in rough form from the start, the user has a good idea of what the finished graphic will look like ultimately. These issues can be resolved by using graphics software as well.

Other graphic elements such as horizontal rules, colored swashes or bars, and clickable icons and buttons can be added to your page to enhance its design. Graphics, icons, and buttons are readily and freely available at scores of sites on the Web. Use them, but also use restraint. Remember, less is more; keep it simple.

WORDS . . . THE FINAL FRONTIER

Of course, none of these wonderful multimedia tools is worth anything if the content is weak or poorly presented. Grammar, punctuation, and spelling errors are just as glaring in cyberspace as they are on paper. If you organize your topics haphazardly, no one will be able to follow you—nor will they want to. If your writing is lifeless, it won't catch or hold anyone's attention. The point is: don't neglect your writing to focus solely on a flashy, multimedia display. Language is still the key to communication, and communication is the key to any publication, paper or electronic.

11 BREAKING THE CODE: PRODUCING A WWW HOME PAGE

What you are creating on the Web is not a single page but a cluster of related pages linked to each other and to external sites. Your home page is the starting point both for you as Web publisher and for your audience as information consumers. Your home page should provide an overview of the purpose and contents of the entire cluster of pages accessible at your site, and it should be straightforward and well organized. It is your top-level page; it presents your face to the public.

Your cluster may offer subject guides, library guides, course descriptions, personal pages for your librarians, and much more. These pages should have an overall unity in appearance and organizing structure. There is room for individuality, but someone visiting several of your pages should be able to readily identify that each is from the same institution. Unifying design elements should be part of the guidelines given to any prospective Web author at your site. (You weren't planning on writing all the pages yourself, were you?) They can be built into template files, which will make everyone's life a bit easier and give everyone a framework within which to work; they will have that much less coding to do. You will receive pages that have consistency embedded within them and will have less editing to do to make them look just right.

As we have noted, a page's appearance depends greatly on the browser being used. While you cannot control the exact appearance of a page because of this, you can design a page so that it will look presentable on most browsers. If you take advantage of formatting features peculiar to a particular browser like Netscape, you should indicate so on the page. That won't make the page look any better on Cello, but at least the Cello user will understand why.

You also need to set up the preferences on your own browser so that you are pleased by both your pages and those you find while exploring the Web as well. You can set up your default fonts, their sizes, the background color, and the colors of your links so that they are easy on your eyes and you like them. You will probably be spending a good portion of your time looking at a wide variety of Web pages from now on, so try to make the experience as pleasant as possible.

Because browsers allow you to open local files not loaded on the Web, you will also be viewing your own pages as you work on them. It is best to write your page (or part of it) and view it on your browser to see how it looks. Then return to your word processor or text editor to edit the file, and view those changes on your browser. Keep both windows open at the same time so you can go back and forth from word processor to browser and get all noticeable problems fixed and cleaned up before you work with your systems administrator in getting files mounted on your Web site. You can even check the links you have set up to make sure they work.

HTML TAGS

How the page looks is all a matter of coding, of applying the Hypertext Markup Language (HTML) codes or tags appropriately. It is not that difficult to create a simple page; HTML tags are fairly basic, although the language continues to expand as new tags and features are created. Tags are all enclosed within brackets such as <H1> and most often are used in pairs, with the second tag indicating the end of a function such as </H1> with a forward slash. HTML is not case sensitive, so <h1> and </h1> mean the same as the above tag example.

Basic tags can be divided into five categories: page division tags, typographic tags, linking tags, listing tags, and multimedia tags. There are other types of tags available that are for more advanced features like forms and Common Gateway Interface (CGI) programming for search indexing. Such advanced features and tags are beyond the scope of this book and are covered in depth by many of the materials in the bibliography in the back.

PAGE DIVISION TAGS

Page division tags are used to identify the different sections of a Web page. They have little real functionality other than to note the structure of the page.

HTML denotes that the page is tagged in HTML. <HTML> goes at the top of your file, and </HTML> goes at the bottom. They do not display on the screen.

Title gives the page name. That name does not display on the page in a graphical browser, but instead displays across the top of the browser's window frame. On a text-based browser, the name appears on the page itself. The protocol is <Title>My Home Page</Title>.

Head and *Body* indicate the head or top of your page and the main body text section of it. Neither displays on the screen. They are used as <Head> head text </Head> <Body> This is the body text of the page . . . </Body>. These tags are used so that Web author can see the page structure more clearly when looking at the HTML coding. Another tool for Web authors is to include programming comments that do not display but may be helpful when editing code. They are placed like this <!— This is a comment —>.

*Address i*s one final page division, although this tag does carry some typographic value. Address is the section of the page where you can list the page's URL, an e-mail address to contact, the name of the Web author, and the date the page was created or last updated. Text between the address tags is generally displayed in italics by graphical browsers. The format is <Address> This page is maintained by John Maxymuk . . . </Address>.

The basic setup of your page can be seen in Figure 11.1. None of these page division tags are absolutely required in order to mount a page on the Web. They are recommended as useful con-

---

FIGURE 11.1 Basic Setup of HTML Page Division Tags

```
<HTML>

<Head>

<Title>

</Title>

</Head>

<Body>

</Body>

<Address>

</Address>

</HTML>
```

ventions, however. Typographic tags are more than just conventions; they give your text its character.

TYPOGRAPHIC TAGS

HTML typographic tags are not nearly as extensive as the typographic controls available from any page-layout program for desktop publishing. These tags come in two basic varieties, logical and physical (see Figure 11.2). How logical tags display on the screen is entirely dependent on how the user's browser is set. Meanwhile, physical tags define how text should be displayed by all browsers. Logical tags include strong, emphasis, cite, and code. Physical tags include bold, italic, and typewriter text.

FIGURE 11.2 HTML Typographic Tags

Typographic Tags

Logical Tags

This text uses the strong tags.

This text uses the emphasis tags.

Cite tags are for *titles of books and films.*

Code tags are used for
```
lines
of
computer
code
```

Physical Tags

This text uses boldface tags.

This text uses italic tags.

```
This text uses typewriter text tags.
```

Strong places strong emphasis on text and is typically displayed in boldface type by most browsers. It is used as <Strong>text</Strong>.

Emphasis also places emphasis on text, but is usually displayed as italic type. It is used as <Em>text</Em>.

Cite is used for titles of books and films and such. Cite text usually displays in italics <Cite>text</Cite>. *Code* is used for displays of computer programming code and is displayed in a fixed-width format similar to typewriter text. <Code>text</Code>

Physical tags mean what they say typographically. *Bold* is used as <B>text</B>. *Italic* is formatted <I>text</I>, and *typewriter text* is applied as <TT>text</TT>. Most of these character-based tags display as underlining in text-based browsers like Lynx.

Heading levels are another form of typographic tag. There are six different levels of headings, and they give a Web author some relative control over point size of type (see Figure 11.3). What heading level 1 means in terms of point size and typeface will vary according to browsers and settings, but it will always be larger type than level two and so forth. Heading level six indicates the smallest type size. This logical tag is applied as <H1>text</H1>, to use level one as an example.

FIGURE 11.3 HTML Heading Levels

HTML HEADINGS

Heading Level One <H1>

Heading Level Two <H2>

Heading Level Three <H3>

Heading Level Four <H4>

Heading Level Five <H5>

Heading Level Six <H6>

Compare the above headings to this normal text.

There are two tags to break up text blocks, line break and paragraph (see Figure 11.4). *Line break* breaks the current line, but does not add a blank line. *Paragraph* ends the current line and does add a blank line. They are used as text
 or text<P>. In that blank space, you may want to include a *horizontal rule* to break up a page or to separate different sections of the page. The horizontal rule sometimes takes the form of a simple line, sometimes a colored bar, sometimes even a row of tiny images. The tag is <HR>.

One other formatting tag is *Preformatted*, which allows you to display ASCII text in the same form as the original, retaining carriage returns, tabs, and spacing. It is applied as <Pre>text to be used</Pre>. It is not recommended to use HTML tags other than links within Preformatted tags. When you choose Preformatted, you shouldn't need any additional page formatting.

Finally, Netscape offers you some additional controls in formatting your page. The *center* function allows you to center graphics or text on the screen. *Font size* allows you to adjust the size of typefaces. The trouble with these is that other browsers will not recognize them. The user needs to be accessing your site with Netscape in order for such tags to have any effect.

LINKING TAGS

Hypertext links are what make pages on the World Wide Web more than just fancy ftp sites; they are the keys to navigation in cyberspace. They are also very simple to construct. The format is

---

FIGURE 11.4 Tools to Break Up a Text Block

Breaking Up Text Blocks

Unformatted text in HTML will wrap from line to line ignoring any ASCII carriage returns in the file. Line break and paragraph are the HTML tags to break up text blocks.

These two lines are broken with the *line break
* tag.
There is no blank line between them.

These two lines are broken with the *paragraph <P>* tag.

There is a blank line between them.

<A HREF="filename or URL">text that will display on the screen</A>. *A* stands for anchor and *HREF* for Hypertext reference. In Figure 10.1, the link *John Maxymuk* connects the user to a Web page called "maxymuk.htm" located in the same file directory as the file for the Librarian page, "libn.htm," on which the link appears. The HTML tag is <A HREF="maxymuk.htm"> John Maxymuk</A>.

Links to files on your own server can be set up as either relative links or absolute pathnames. Relative links do not give the full URL for a link, because the link is generally in the same directory on the same machine as the Web page itself. Relative links are recommended because they are shorter and do not change if all your pages are moved to a new server. Absolute pathnames use the full URL of the link. The John Maxymuk link above is a relative link. To use absolute pathnames would make the construction <A HREF="http://www.rutgers.edu/rulibs/camden/ maxymuk.htm">John Maxymuk</A>.

You can link to far-flung resources through the use of URLs. The resources could be other Web pages, **ftp** sites or files, **telnet** sites, **usenet** readers, or **wais** servers. Anything that can be specified in a URL can be linked on a Web page. To provide a link to the Yahoo Web indexing server, you would enter it this way: <A HREF="http://www.yahoo.com/">Yahoo</A>.

For longer, multiscreen documents, you might want to set up a table of contents at the top of the page that allows you to jump to links set up several lines or screens down the page. Setting up this type of link is a two-step process. First, you set up your anchor name; perhaps it is "Section II." You would tag that text as <A NAME="linkname">Section II</A>. Second, you set up your table of contents link with a link called something like "Go to Section II." In your coding that would be written as <A HREF="#linkname">Go To Section II</A>.

One other useful type of link is a mailto link. A mailto link allows you to include an e-mail address as a link on your page so that users can easily send comments to you, assuming that their browsers are set up to handle mailto links. The protocol to list my e-mail address in a mailto link would be <A HREF= "mailto:maxymuk@zodiac.rutgers.edu">maxymuk@zodiac. rutgers. edu</A>.

There are two keys to designing good links. One, make sure the link is a useful, reliable, accessible site for your user to visit. If the link takes the user to a site where there is nothing of particular interest, the user will doubt the usefulness of your page as well. If the link has moved or vanished or is often unavailable or exceedingly slow, then that will also reflect badly on your page.

Second, the wording of the link should be succinct and flow naturally in the general content of the page. Don't say, "Click here for policies on collection development." Instead try, "Policies on collection development are available."

LIST TAGS

One common way to format information on the Web is in lists. Lists can be tagged in several ways: unnumbered, numbered, and definition (see Figure 11.5). Each formats the display of the listed information a little differently.

The tags for an *unnumbered list* are <UL> </UL>, and each item in the list is preceded by the tag <LI>, which stands for "list item." An unnumbered list of library departments would be tagged:

```
<UL>
<LI> Reference
<LI> Circulation
<LI> Technical Services
</UL>
```

A *numbered list* is exactly the same except that it displays numbers and uses the tags <OL> </OL>. On text-based browsers like Lynx, all lists essentially become numbered lists.

```
<OL>
<LI> Reference
<LI> Circulation
<LI> Technical Services
</OL>
```

A *definition list* is constructed with the tags definition list <DL> </DL>, definition term <DT>, and definition <DD>. It provides a hanging indent appearance to the text display.

```
<DL>
<DT> Reference
<DD> The Reference Department answers questions posed in person, over the telephone or by e-mail. The telephone number for Reference is 999-9999.
</DL>
```

List tags sometimes can be used to provide indented text formatting.

FIGURE 11.5 HTML List Tags

List Tags

Unnumbered List

☐ Reference
☐ Circulation
☐ Technical Services

Numbered List

1. Reference
2. Circulation
3. Technical Services

Definition List

Reference
    The Reference Department answers questions posed in person, over the telephone or by e-mail.
    The telephone number is...
Circulation
    The Circulation Department...
Technical Services
    Technical Services...

MULTIMEDIA TAGS

Multimedia tags include those for graphics, sound files, and movies. Graphics are divided into in-line images, which are incorporated with the text on the page, and external images, which must be chosen from the page and then will load as their own page. Sound files and movies are also externally based and require that your browser include the appropriate player files.

Most in-line images are either GIF or JPEG files (described in chapter 10). The format of the tag is <IMG SRC="filename.gif">. If the image is a JPEG file, then the extension would be .jpg instead of .gif. To add an alternative for text-based browsers, so that a phrase will be displayed in place of the image, use <IMG SRC="filename.gif" ALT"This is a photo of the library.">

In-line images can also be displayed so that the top, bottom, or middle of the image is aligned with the accompanying text (see Figure 11.6). The format to align the bottom of the image with the text is <IMG Align=bottom SRC="filename.gif">. To align top or middle, simply replace the word bottom with either term in the tag.

FIGURE 11.6 Aligning In-Line Images

Aligning In-Line Images with Text

Align Bottom

The bottom of this image is aligned with this line of text.

Align Middle

The middle of this image is aligned with this line of text.

Align Top

The top of this image is aligned with this line of text.

External images and sound files and movies all use an anchor tag. A typical tag for an external JPEG image would be <A HREF="filename.jpg">Here's an image.</A> If the image file is in a different directory on your server or on a different server entirely, then you would need the absolute path, the full URL. The construction for other multimedia files would differ only in the filename extension. A sound file might be .au or .aiff; a movie might be .mpg or .mov. There are many other multimedia format possibilities.

Many other more advanced features of HTML and Web pages are beyond the scope of this book's attention to the Web. The bibliography provides a selection of resources that detail such features as image maps, access counters, CGI programming, using forms, creating tables, setting up audio files and movies, blinking text, fade-in titles, and the use of backgrounds. Not to mention Java.

SETTING UP A BASIC HOME PAGE

Now that you're familiar with the simplest HTML codes, you can set up a page. Use the page division tags (HTML, Head, Title, Body, Address) to set up your page. With these as your guide, you can work on the four main parts of any page: the nameplate or page banner, the main body, the signature or address, and the navigation control area.

As an example to show how simple this is, we'll create a home page for the mythical Mudville Public Library. The figures in this section are presented in pairs, one showing the HTML coding and the other showing the Netscape browser display.

PAGE BANNER

The page banner or nameplate of a home page serves an identifying function just as the nameplate does for newsletters and library guides. It should be attractive, distinctive, and set the tone for your site. Page banners usually are a combination of text and graphics, especially for home pages. If your organization has a logo, this is a good place to put it. For subordinate pages, you may choose just to run a topical header identifying the purpose of the page and save the space taken up by the graphic and home page header. Or you may run the topical header of the subordinate page as a second-level heading beneath the home page banner.

Graphics for the banner can be created with graphics software packages if you have a computer graphics artist on staff; alternatively, you can commission your computing services department to create one—if you have such a department. If you are on a tight budget, like the Mudville Public, you can search the Web for usable public domain click art. There are scores of sites with freely available images, icons, buttons, bullets, bars, and more. Try a Web indexer like Yahoo. That's how I found the image and dividing bar in Figures 11.7 and 11.8. (Specifically, the image is from http://seidel.ncsa.uiuc.edu/ClipArt/cmu-english-server.html/ and the bar is from http://www.econ.cbs.dk/people/nagelmal/psyched/index.html.)

This page is left aligned, like most pages on the Web. Netscape offers a centering tag, but other browsers will not recognize it, so this page is designed with that in mind. The bar provides a physical division of the page, just as we have structurally separated the page banner from the main body. This page also includes the ALT tag so that those with text-based browsers can easily read the page.

MAIN BODY

The main body of the page contains the content, the message you want to communicate to users. On a home page it is likely to function as a table of contents or organizing structure to the information you have gathered on your cluster of pages. On our

FIGURE 11.7 Page Banner for Mudville Public

FIGURE 11.8 HTML Coding for Figure 11.7

```
<HTML>

<Head>

<Title>Mudville Public Library Home Page</Title>

</Head>

<Body>

<H1><IMG ALT="Image of the Mighty Casey." Align=bottom

SRC="casey.gif">Mudville Public Library</H1>

<IMG SRC="bar.gif">

</Body>

<Address>

</Address>

</HTML>
```

Mudville example, the body of the home page includes a short welcoming paragraph outlining the scope of the site and a subject-arrangement list of links to subordinate pages (see Figures 11.9 and 11.10).

The main body section of each subordinate page will cover what's indicated here. Subordinate pages will provide access to the library catalog, indexes the library makes available electronically, subject guides of links to other Internet resources, information on librarians, collections, branches, hours, and whatever else suits the imagination of your organization.

SIGNATURE

This area of the page is for establishing origin and authorship data roughly equivalent to the masthead of a newsletter (see Figures 11.11 and 11.12). Signing your page adds a certain amount of validity to the information contained on it; unsigned pages are less authoritative. Every page should be signed at the bottom so that the Web author or person responsible for updates can be contacted easily by the user. The person to contact with sugges-

FIGURE 11.9 Page Banner and Main Body for Mudville Public

 **Mudville Public Library**

The Mudville Public Library exists primarily to serve the needs of community residents, but its physical and electronic doors are open to all interested parties. Our special collection of baseball literature is of particular note, and our archives of Mighty Casey memorabilia are available to researchers.

- **Hours, Location and Staff**
- **Online Catalog**
- **Mighty Casey Archives**

tions or comments should be listed here, as should the date of the last page revision and the copyright status of the page. The signature area also should include the URL of the page because that will not necessarily be included on the printout generated by the user's browser. Including the URL at the very bottom of the page will ensure that if a user prints a page from your site, the URL will be at hand if he or she would like to revisit it later. The signature area also is a good place to put the logo of your organization if you did not already put it in your page banner.

NAVIGATION CONTROLS

Navigation controls provide an easy way for users to jump around your cluster of pages, whether it be up a level, to the home page, to the previous or next page, or even to a page set up to receive user comments (see Figures 11.13 and 11.14). Navigation controls can either be textual or graphical. Graphic navigation controls such as icons and buttons are more attractive and eye-catching to someone using a graphical browser, but a text alternative needs to be present for Lynx users.

FIGURE 11.10 Added HTML Coding for Figure 11.9

```
<HTML>
<Head>
<Title>Mudville Public Library Home Page</Title>
</Head>
<Body>
<H1><IMG ALT="Image of the Mighty Casey." Align=bottom
SRC="casey.gif">Mudville Public Library</H1>
<IMG SRC="bar.gif"><P>

The Mudville Public Library exists primarily to serve the needs
of community residents, but its physical and electronic doors are
open to all interested parties.  Our special collection of
baseball literature is of particular note, and our archives of
Mighty Casey memorabilia are available to researchers.<P>

<UL><H2>
<LI><A HREF="http://www.casey.mudville.net/mud.html">Hours,
Location and Staff</A>
<LI><A HREF="telnet://casey.mudville.net">Online Catalog</A>
<LI><A HREF="http://www.casey.mudville.net/casey.html">Mighty
Casey Archives</A>
</H2></UL>
</Body>
<Address>
</Address>
</HTML>
```

These controls can be placed immediately above the signature area, at the very bottom of the page, at the very top of the page, or at both the very bottom and top of the page. If your pages are lengthy, navigation controls at the top of the page can save the user time if he or she quickly sees that this page is not of interest. Navigation controls are essential on subordinate pages, but not for home pages, since the user is already at the top level. Icons, buttons, and button bars are all available freely from the same sorts of sites noted in the above section on page banners.

Constructing a simple Web page is as easy as demonstrated in the above Mudville example. Once you've created a few, you might want to consult some of the sources in the bibliography to learn about more advanced features to include on your pages. However, in the next chapter, we'll continue with our simple home page and discuss fine-tuning it, getting it on the Web, and making users aware of it.

FIGURE 11.11 Page Banner, Main Body, and Signature for Mudville Public

Mudville Public Library

The Mudville Public Library exists primarily to serve the needs of community residents, but its physical and electronic doors are open to all interested parties. Our special collection of baseball literature is of particular note, and our archives of Mighty Casey memorabilia are available to researchers.

- **Hours, Location and Staff**
- **Online Catalog**
- **Mighty Casey Archives**

http://www.casey.mudville.net/fig1111.htm
Last updated January 1, 1996 by John Maxymuk

Please e-mail any comments or suggestions to:
maxymuk@zodiac.rutgers.edu

FIGURE 11.12 Added HTML Coding for Figure 11.11

```
<HTML>
<Head>
<Title>Mudville Public Library Home Page</Title>
</Head>
<Body>
<H1><IMG ALT="Image of the Mighty Casey." Align=bottom
SRC="casey.gif">Mudville Public Library</H1>
<IMG SRC="bar.gif"><P>

The Mudville Public Library exists primarily to serve the needs
of community residents, but its physical and electronic doors are
open to all interested parties.  Our special collection of
baseball literature is of particular note, and our archives of
Mighty Casey memorabilia are available to researchers.<P>

<UL><H2>
<LI><A HREF="http://www.casey.mudville.net/mud.html">Hours,
Location and Staff</A>
<LI><A HREF="telnet://casey.mudville.net">Online Catalog</A>
<LI><A HREF="http://www.casey.mudville.net/casey.html">Mighty
Casey Archives</A>
</H2></UL>
</Body>
<IMG SRC="bar.gif"><P>
<Address>http://www.casey.mudville.net/fig1111.htm<BR>
Last updated January 1, 1996 by John Maxymuk<P>
Please e-mail any comments or suggestions to:<BR>
<A
HREF="mailto:maxymuk@zodiac.rutgers.edu">maxymuk@zodiac.rutgers.e
du</A>
</Address>
</HTML>
```

FIGURE 11.13 Subordinate Page with Icon Navigation Controls

The Correspondence of the Mighty Casey

The archives of Mighty Casey memorabilia contain a complete collection of all known correspondence of Casey. The <u>letters</u> were collected and maintained by Casey's friend and celebrant, <u>Ernest L. Thayer</u>.

Back to Home Page **Back to Casey Archives**

http://www.casey.mudville.net/fig1113.htm
Last updated January 1, 1996 by John Maxymuk

Please e-mail any comments or suggestions to:
maxymuk@crab.rutgers.edu

FIGURE 11.14 HTML Coding for Figure 11.13

```
<HTML>
<Head>
<Title>Mighty Casey Letters</Title>
</Head>
<Body>
<H1>The Correspondence of the Mighty Casey</H1>
<IMG HEIGHT=40 WIDTH=637 SRC="bar.gif"><P>

The archives of Mighty Casey memorabilia contain a complete
collection of all known correspondence of Casey.  The <A
HREF="http://www.casey.mudville.net/letters.html">letters</A>
were collected and maintained by Casey's friend and celebrant, <A
HREF="http://www.casey.mudville.net/Thayer.html">Ernest L.
Thayer</A>.<P>

</Body>
<HR><P>
<IMG HEIGHT=50 WIDTH=48 SRC="casey.gif"><Strong>Back to Home
Page</Strong>
<IMG HEIGHT=50 WIDTH=48 SRC="books.gif"><Strong>Back to Casey
Archives</Strong>
<HR><P>
<Address>http://www.casey.mudville.net/fig1113.htm<BR>
Last updated January 1, 1996 by John Maxymuk<P>
Please e-mail any comments or suggestions to:<BR>
<A
HREF="mailto:maxymuk@zodiac.rutgers.edu">maxymuk@crab.rutgers.edu
</A>
</Address>
</HTML>
```

12 THIS SITE UNDER CONSTRUCTION: PUBLISHING A HOME PAGE ON THE WORLD WIDE WEB

The clear distinctions between printed publications and Web pages both in planning and production hold true for the publication stage as well. Once a newsletter is published, it's done and can't be changed. Grammatical mistakes or bad layout decisions are there forever. Try to improve the next issue. Library guides are a little different in that they should be regularly updated, but that regularity might mean once every year or two or until the print run is exhausted.

The Web is not static. On the Web, publishing a page can be practically a daily occurrence depending on how much time the Web author has to devote. While the workload involved in trying to keep a Web page or cluster of pages up-to-date can be fierce, mistakes of spelling, grammar, or punctuation can be quickly corrected and bad design decisions can be readily fixed.

TESTING THE PAGE

Even though it is simple to correct mistakes after first publication, it is best to avoid obvious errors from the start. The key to getting things right is testing. As you create your page(s), you will be jumping back and forth from your text editor to your browser. This will give you ample opportunity to observe how your page will appear on the Web to people using the same browser as you. Differences will arise from how they have set the options on that same browser, but the view will be essentially the same.

For those using another browser, the look can be wholly different—particularly for those using text-based browsers. The figures in chapter 10 illustrated how Netscape, Mosaic, and Lynx might display the very same HTML coding. What you should do is test your pages on a variety of browsers so you can alleviate any significant problems that arise on different platforms. A variation in the look is to be expected, but it should not be hideous or make the page less functional.

The browsers you use to test view your pages will depend on which ones you have easy access to and which ones your target audience is likely to be using. If you are with an academic library, your target audience is more likely to be closely defined, and its most popular browsers are more likely to be known. Other libraries targeting a more diverse public are less likely to have a clear idea of what browsers their public is using. At the very least, you will want to test your pages on Netscape, Mosaic, and Lynx.

If you have a friend or colleague who uses another browser you don't have access to, then you can ask them to critique the look of your page on that browser. Better yet, ask them to print out the screens of your pages for you; bear in mind a printout will not show any color on your page. Assuming that your page has some features users will want to retain in a paper copy, it's a good idea to test print from your browser(s) as well. The paperless society has not yet arrived.

Test all the links on your pages. Try all of the navigation controls. Proofread for typographical errors. Check the quality of the writing. Make sure the organization of the information on the pages makes sense. You're now ready to mount the pages on your server.

MOUNTING THE FILES

Mounting simply means transferring the files that comprise your pages to the server from which any WWW user can access them. Your pages partly consist of text files of HTML coding. (If you've used a word processor to create these pages, make sure you save the files as ASCII text files and not as WordPerfect or Word files.) In addition, your pages consist of any additional graphic, sound, or movie files that give your pages their multimedia flavor.

Text files should have a .htm or .html extension. Multimedia files will vary according to format; they could be .gif, .jpg, .au, .mpg, or many others. Many Web servers use the Unix operating system, which is case sensitive. For this reason, you may want to make your filenames all lower case for consistency and to make your pages more user friendly. A user may want to add your page as a link on his or her page or to connect directly to your site rather than through an automated link. If your filename is a mix of upper and lower case, there is a greater chance of error and of no connection being established.

You will transfer your files to your Web server's public directory. That server may belong to your computing services department or to an Internet service provider to which your organization subscribes. You need to discuss any restrictions to or requirements of maintaining a Web site on that server with the systems administrator. You may be able to set up an alias for your server so that the URL of your pages will remain the same even if the actual machine the server is on changes. You may also want to set up a Webmaster alias for yourself to serve as a repository for e-mail regarding your Web pages.

In order to maintain your Web pages, you will need to perform some rudimentary operations in the Unix environment of your server from time to time. You may need to use basic Unix commands to rename files, create new directories, move files to new directories, or delete old files.

You probably will transfer those files to your server using a form of ftp (the file transfer protocol for the Internet). You need to know how to log in to the server, where to load your files, and what transfer program to use. It may be a very primitive ftp program or a more user-friendly menu-driven version. In either case, you need to specify the files to transfer and how you want them transferred. For the .html text files, you will not need to specify a special transfer method. However, for multimedia files, you will need to specify that they be transferred as binary files. Otherwise they will not be uploaded to the server in a usable form. Once you've transferred the files and placed them in their proper directories as per your Web server's requirements, your site is open for business.

Basic Unix Commands

cd ..	Changes directory to parent directory.
cd /newdirectory	Changes directory to specified new directory.
cp filename /newdirectory	Copies file to specified new directory
ls	Lists contents of directory.
man command	Provides help screens for specified command.
mkdir newdir	Makes a new directory with the specified name.
mv oldfile newfile	Renames specified file.
pwd	Prints name of current ("working") directory.
rm filename	Deletes specified file.

PUBLICIZING THE SITE

Your site may be open for business, but how will anyone know? You want visitors; you probably have a target audience in mind. How do you notify them?

The first thing you might do is post a notice on any **listservs** that are concerned with information supplied on your pages. A wider form of electronic publicity can be garnered by registering with several of the Web indexing services. These include:

Lycos	http://www.lycos.com/addasite.html
NCSA	http://www.ncsa.uiuc.edu/SDG/ Software/Mosaic/Docs/what's-new- form.html
WebCrawler	http://webcrawler.com/WebCrawler/ SubmitURLS.html
World Wide Web Worm	http://wwwmcb.cs.colorado.edu/ home/mcbryan/WWWWadd.html
Yahoo	http://www.yahoo.com/text/bin/add

These services all provide forms with which you can register your site so that users can find it with a subject searching mechanism.

Print publicity is also useful, particularly for a local target audience. Put a notice in any newsletters put out by your organization or in any you know your target audience reads. Prepare a library guide that outlines how to access the new site. Put the site's URL on your business card and in the signature file of your e-mail. List that URL anywhere you think your audience will see it.

TROUBLESHOOTING

Once your site is open for business, what's the first thing to do? Testing, of course. These are living pages, so the need for testing never ceases. In particular, when your page is brand new you'll want to make sure that everything looks right and works. Test periodically and test at different times of day. That link you added when you revised the page at 2 A.M. may be so busy during the middle of the day as to be virtually inaccessible. Users are looking for pages that provide value, ones that are well organized and up-to-date. It's your responsibility to make sure that happens.

Learn the HTML tags thoroughly; many common errors are the result of sloppy coding. Overlapping tags such as

<H1>This is a <B>header</H1>with overlapping bold.</B>

may make your page display differently from what you intended. Perhaps what you intended was

<H1>This is a <B>header</B> without overlapping bold.</H1>.

Incomplete pairs of quotes or tags are two examples of sloppy coding that can lead to nonfunctioning tags. Don't forget the closing quotation mark at the end of a Hypertext reference tag like this—<A HREF="/filename.gif>. Close it like this <A HREF="/ filename.gif">.

Likewise, don't neglect the end tag for any pair of tags like this:

Only this *word should be in emphasized text, but without an ending tag, emphasized text does not stop.*

Remember the ending tag in this case would be .

Paragraph break errors are also common. A paragraph break can be used to introduce white space onto a page (as well as separate paragraphs), but it should not be used in certain cases where the tags already denote a break. Tags for headings, addresses, list items, and preformatted text all imply a paragraph break. You don't need to supply a <p> before or after them.

Above all, keep learning. HTML is the language of desktop publishing for the Web, and it is an evolving one. Master the basics outlined in this book, and then read further. Don't stop here; there are many more advanced features you can tackle.

MENDING LINKS

Links are the preferred mode of navigation across the WWW, so if they are not functioning your user hits a dead end. Make that navigation clear for both graphical and text-based browsers. Don't use "click here" as your link; instead have the link be part of the natural wording of the text. In addition, remember that most Web sites are Unix based and case sensitive, so get those URLs right, both the characters and the case.

Make sure that the URL of the link is formatted correctly. If the link is to a directory or site rather than an .html file, include a **trailing** slash "/" after the directory or site name. That will make it easier for your browser to find the site you are looking for.

Also be aware that access to some sites is restricted to certain types of users or times of the day. Make sure that most of your users can connect to your link at most times of the day. If not, make a note of it on your page or delete the link.

If the link is to a specific location on your own page, make sure that the names in the target marker and the destination tags match. Otherwise, when the user clicks on the destination tag, the browser will not find the target marker, and the link will not work. Finally, don't forget to check your mailto link. If no mail form pops up, your browser may not be set up to support mail forms. If it pops up, but you receive no mail, the address might be wrong or badly formatted.

FINE-TUNING YOUR DESIGN

The WWW is a vehicle for sharing related information quickly and efficiently. The design of your page should reflect this quintessential concept. Information should be well displayed, well organized, and well connected; use the Hypertext capabilities of the medium to their fullest. Link to external sites or files of relevant interest. Provide links to target markers set up within your page if it is lengthy. Set up a navigation control bar so that users can quickly jump to a higher level, the next page, or back to the home page.

Maintain your style and format both on an individual page and across all pages on a server. Keep the basic layout of all your pages the same and offer the same navigational features from each. Don't overdo the use of typographic tags and features like boldface, italics, and font sizes. Use heading levels in order (<H1> first, then <H2>, and so forth), and don't use all levels on each page. Ensure that you construct your tags correctly and consistently. One common error is to leave space immediately following the beginning tag and immediately before the ending tag. The result, especially in links, can be unattractive.

Backgrounds can be used to add color or a clever design to your page, but make sure the text is easily readable on your background. Don't make backgrounds too dark, too busy, or so large in bytes that the user's access time will suffer appreciably. A similar criterion can be applied for any of the more flashy effects possible on the Web, like blinking text or fade-ins. If the effect does not accent the message and make the information more easily read and understood, then skip it.

Figure 12.1 illustrates some bad design elements (see Figure 12.2 for the HTML coding). The page in the figures uses an abundance of typographic tags and too many out of order headings. The link tags are not formatted correctly, and there are no navigation controls. See Figures 12.3 and 12.4 for the improvements.

FASHIONING GRAPHICS

Of course, you want to take advantage of the multimedia capabilities of the Web. If your site is for an art museum library, then your content dictates the inclusion of numerous graphics of paintings and other works of art. But for another type of library, a heavy use of images may be highly tangential and irrelevant. In that case, in-line images should be held to a minimum so as to improve the layout and accent the page's content.

In the interests of users, in-line graphics should be small and far between. Large and numerous graphics significantly slow the loading speed of your page whether the user has an ethernet connection or a 14.4 modem. Speed is a significant factor for users. Try to make your page as quick to load as possible. If you provide a link to an image, try to have the image file reside on your server and not elsewhere on the Web.

Furthermore, images should be of good visual quality, sized for

---

FIGURE 12.1 WWW Page with Design Problems

A Few *Helpful* WWW Sites...

Guides to Using HTML

- ☐ A Beginner's Guide to HTML
- ☐ Composing Good HTML
- ☐ Don Siegel's Tips
- ☐ How Do They Do That With HTML?
- ☐ How to Publish on the World Wide Web
- ☐ HTML Bad Style Page
- ☐ The HTML Writers Guild: Principles of Good HTML Design
- ☐ The Only HTML Information Page You Really Need
- ☐ Putting Information on the Web

And if you are looking for the *mother of all* repositories click here for Yahoo's listing of World Wide Web Resources.

FIGURE 12.2 HTML Coding for Figure 12.1

```
<HTML>
<Head><Title>HTML Guides</Title>
</Head>

<Body><H2>A Few <em>Helpful</em> WWW Sites...</H2>
<H1>Guides to Using HTML</H1>

<UL>
<LI><A
HREF="http://www.ncsa.uiuc.edu/General/Internet/WWW/HTMLPrimer.ht
ml">  A Beginner's Guide to HTML  </A>
<LI><A HREF="http://www.cs.cmu.edu/~tilt/cgh/">  Composing Good
HTML  </A>
<LI><A HREF="http://www.best.com/~DSiegel/tips/">  Don Siegel's
Tips  </A>
<LI><A
HREF="http://www.nashville.net/~carl/htmlguide/index.html">  How
Do They Do That With HTML?  </A>
<LI><A HREF="http://www.thegiim.org">  How to Publish on the
World Wide Web  </A>
<LI><A HREF="http://www.earth.com/bad-style">  HTML Bad Style
Page  </A>
<LI><A
HREF="http://ugweb.cs.ualberta.ca/~gerald/guild/style.html">  The
HTML Writers Guild: Principles of Good HTML Design  </A>
<LI><A HREF="http://www.ocala.com/~bombadil/nuthin/yahoo.htm">
The Only HTML Information Page You Really Need  </A>
<LI><A
HREF="http://www.w3.org/hypertext/WWW/Provider/Overview.html">
Putting Information on the Web  </A>
</UL>

<strong>And if you are looking for the <em>mother of
all</em> repositories click <A
HREF="http://www.yahoo.com/Computers_and_Internet/Internet/World_
Wide_Web">  here</A> for Yahoo's listing of World Wide Web
Resources.</strong>

</Body>
</HTML>
```

FIGURE 12.3 Redesigned Figure 12.1

Guides to Using HTML

- ☐ <u>A Beginner's Guide to HTML</u>
- ☐ <u>Composing Good HTML</u>
- ☐ <u>Don Siegel's Tips</u>
- ☐ <u>How Do They Do That With HTML?</u>
- ☐ <u>How to Publish on the World Wide Web</u>
- ☐ <u>HTML Bad Style Page</u>
- ☐ <u>The HTML Writers Guild: Principles of Good HTML Design</u>
- ☐ <u>The Only HTML Information Page You Really Need</u>
- ☐ <u>Putting Information on the Web</u>

The mother of all repositories is <u>Yahoo's listing of World Wide Web Resources</u>.

**Back to Home Page** **Back to Previous Level**

http://www.casey.mudville.net/fig123.htm
Last updated January 1, 1996 by John Maxymuk

Please e-mail any comments or suggestions to:
<u>*maxymuk@crab.rutgers.edu*</u>

---

best effect, and cropped so that nonessential elements don't detract from the focus of the image. Figures 12.5 and 12.6 demonstrate a poor use of graphics (see Figure 12.7 for the HTML coding). The images on the page are both too large and too numerous as well as haphazardly placed. They overwhelm the layout of the page and detract from the textual information. The images themselves are mostly of little interest and are not cropped for proper emphasis. What works better? See Figures 12.8, 12.9, and 12.10.

MAINTAINING YOUR PUBLICATION

As has been frequently emphasized in this section, a WWW site needs to be kept current. The information and text should be checked constantly for accuracy and freshness. Links should be checked to make sure they are still active, correct, and worthwhile. In your ongoing research of the Web, you will find new information and links of interest to add to your page. Periodically, these changes and new resources can be so numerous that the whole organization of your server may need to change.

Even if the changes are minor ones to a few links on a page, the revising process may be much more complicated than you might realize. If you remove a link from page A, it may affect page B. Proceed carefully and keep track of your pages. If you need to insert a new page onto your server, then major changes are in order. You must fit that new page into the cluster by linking from it to existing pages and from existing pages back to the new page. Code may need to be cut and pasted from one page to another and must fit into existing coding. And then all the pages need to be tested again.

Finally, monitor the use of your page. Ask your systems administrator how you can check your server's log files. From these you can see what pages are being read and which aren't. You can tell also what types of users are coming to your site. Are they from .edu (educational) addresses or from .com (commercial) addresses? Does this match your projected target audience? How does this knowledge of your audience and the reception of your message jibe with the mission of your Web presence? What changes do you need to make? This isn't the Bible, the Koran, or Shakespeare. No Web page is permanent. Publishing on the Web is recording a timely status report on the ether of cyberspace.

FIGURE 12.4 HTML Coding for Figure 12.3

```
<HTML>
<Head><Title>HTML Guides</Title></Head>

<Body>
<H1>Guides to Using HTML</H1><HR>

<UL>
<LI><A
HREF="http://www.ncsa.uiuc.edu/General/Internet/WWW/HTMLPrimer.ht
ml">A Beginner's Guide to HTML</A>
<LI><A HREF="http://www.cs.cmu.edu/~tilt/cgh/">Composing Good
HTML</A>
<LI><A HREF="http://www.best.com/~dsiegel/tips/">Don Siegel's
Tips</A>
<LI><A
HREF="http://www.nashville.net/~carl/htmlguide/index.html">How Do
They Do That With HTML?</A>
<LI><A HREF="http://www.thegiim.org/">How to Publish on the World
Wide Web</A>
<LI><A HREF="http://www.earth.com/bad-style/">HTML Bad Style
Page</A>
<LI><A
HREF="http://ugweb.cs.ualberta.ca/~gerald/guild/style.html">The
HTML Writers Guild: Principles of Good HTML Design</A>
<LI><A HREF="http://www.ocala.com/~bombadil/nuthin/yahoo.htm">The
Only HTML Information Page You Really Need</A>
<LI><A
HREF="http://www.w3.org/hypertext/WWW/Provider/Overview.html"
>Putting Information on the Web</A>
</UL>
The mother of all repositories is <A
HREF="http://www.yahoo.com/Computers_and_Internet/Internet/World_
Wide_Web">Yahoo's listing of World Wide Web Resources</A>.
</Body>
<HR><P>

<IMG HEIGHT=50 WIDTH=48 SRC="h.gif"><Strong>Back to Home
Page</Strong>
<IMG HEIGHT=50 WIDTH=48 SRC="door1.gif"><Strong>Back to Previous
Level</Strong><P>

<Address>http://www.casey.mudville.net/fig123.htm<BR>
Last updated January 1, 1996 by John Maxymuk<P>
Please e-mail any comments or suggestions to:<BR>
<A
HREF="mailto:maxymuk@crab.rutgers.edu">maxymuk@crab.rutgers.edu
</A></Address>

</HTML>
```

FIGURE 12.5 Graphically Unappealing WWW Page

A Few Helpful WWW Sites of Note...

- ☐ <u>DTP by Lee</u>
- ☐ <u>DTP Internet Jump List</u>
- ☐ <u>GetInfo DTP Online Newsletter</u>

FIGURE 12.5 (cont.)

☐ <u>Will-Harris House</u>
☐ <u>Yahoo's listing of Desktop Publishing Resources</u>.

 **Back to Home Page**

http://www.casey.mudville.net/fig125.htm
Last updated January 1, 1996 by John Maxymuk

Please e-mail any comments or suggestions to:
maxymuk@crab.rutgers.edu

FIGURE 12.6 Lynx Version of Figure 12.5

Desktop Publishing Resources on the Web (p1 of 2)

[IMAGE]

A FEW HELPFUL WWW SITES OF NOTE...

[IMAGE]
  * [1]DTP by Lee
  * [2]DTP Internet Jump List
  * [3]GetInfo DTP Online Newsletter
  * [4]Will-Harris House [IMAGE]
  * [5]Yahoo's listing of Desktop Publishing Resources.

[IMAGE]

-- press space for next page --
  Arrow keys: Up and Down to move. Right to follow a link; Left to go back.
  H)elp O)ptions P)rint G)o M)ain screen Q)uit /=search [delete]=history list
± pisces   02 25

Desktop Publishing Resources on the Web (p2 of 2)

[IMAGE] Back to Home Page

http://www.casey.mudville.net/fig125.htm
Last updated January 1, 1996 by John Maxymuk

Please e-mail any comments or suggestions to:
[6]maxymuk@crab.rutgers.edu

Commands: Use arrow keys to move, '?' for help, 'q' to quit, '<-' to go back
  Arrow keys: Up and Down to move. Right to follow a link; Left to go back.
  H)elp O)ptions P)rint G)o M)ain screen Q)uit /=search [delete]=history list
± pisces   02:25

FIGURE 12.7 HTML Coding for Figure 12.5

```
<HTML>
<Head><Title>Desktop Publishing Resources on the Web</Title>
</Head>
<Body>
<IMG SRC="desktop.gif"><P>
<H1>A Few Helpful WWW Sites of Note...</H1><HR><P>
<IMG SRC="pc1.gif">
<UL>
<LI><A HREF="http://www.oo.com/~bennett/">DTP by Lee</A>
<LI><A HREF="http://www.cs.purdue.edu/homes/gwp/dtp/dtp.html">DTP
Internet Jump List</A>
<LI><A HREF="http://www.winternet.com/~jmg/Getinfo.html">GetInfo
DTP Online Newsletter</A>
<LI><A HREF="http://www.will-harris.com/whh.htm">Will-Harris
House</A>
<IMG SRC="pen_ink.gif"><LI><A
HREF="http://www.yahoo.com/Computers_and_Internet/Desktop_Publish
ing">Yahoo's listing of Desktop Publishing Resources</A>.
</Body>
</UL><IMG SRC="printer1.gif">
<HR><P>

<IMG HEIGHT=50 WIDTH=48 SRC="h.gif"><Strong>Back to Home
Page</Strong><P>

<Address>http://www.casey.mudville.net/fig125.htm<BR>
Last updated January 1, 1996 by John Maxymuk<P>
Please e-mail any comments or suggestions to:<BR>
<A
HREF="mailto:maxymuk@crab.rutgers.edu">maxymuk@crab.rutgers.edu
</A></Address>
</HTML>
```

FIGURE 12.8 Better Use of Graphics

A Few Helpful WWW Sites of Note...

- ☐ <u>DTP by Lee</u>
- ☐ <u>DTP Internet Jump List</u>
- ☐ <u>GetInfo DTP Online Newsletter</u>
- ☐ <u>Will-Harris House</u>
- ☐ <u>Yahoo's listing of Desktop Publishing Resources</u>.

**Back to Home Page**

http://www.casey.mudville.net/fig128.htm
Last updated January 1, 1996 by John Maxymuk

Please e-mail any comments or suggestions to:
<u>maxymuk@crab.rutgers.edu</u>

FIGURE 12.9 Lynx Version of Figure 12.8

Desktop Publishing Resources on the Web (p1 of 2)

[IMAGE]

A FEW HELPFUL WWW SITES OF NOTE...

_____

* [1]DTP by Lee
* [2]DTP Internet Jump List
* [3]GetInfo DTP Online Newsletter
* [4]Will-Harris House
* [5]Yahoo's listing of Desktop Publishing Resources.

[IMAGE]

_____

-- press space for next page --
  Arrow keys: Up and Down to move. Right to follow a link; Left to go back.
 H)elp O)ptions P)rint G)o M)ain screen Q)uit /=search [delete]=history list
± pisces   02 20

Desktop Publishing Resources on the Web (p2 of 2)

[IMAGE] Back to Home Page

  http://www.casey.mudville.net/fig128.htm
  Last updated January 1, 1996 by John Maxymuk

  Please e-mail any comments or suggestions to:
  [6]maxymuk@crab.rutgers.edu

Commands: Use arrow keys to move, '?' for help, 'q' to quit, '<-' to go back
  Arrow keys: Up and Down to move. Right to follow a link; Left to go back.
 H)elp O)ptions P)rint G)o M)ain screen Q)uit /=search [delete]=history list
± pisces   02 20

FIGURE 12.10 HTML Coding for Figure 12.8

```
<HTML>
<Head><Title>Desktop Publishing Resources on the Web</Title>
</Head>

<Body>
<IMG SRC="desktop.gif"><P>

<H1>A Few Helpful WWW Sites of Note...</H1><HR><P>

<UL>
<LI><A HREF="http://www.oo.com/~bennett/">DTP by Lee</A>
<LI><A HREF="http://www.cs.purdue.edu/homes/gwp/dtp/dtp.html">DTP
Internet Jump List</A>
<LI><A HREF="http://www.winternet.com/~jmg/Getinfo.html">GetInfo
DTP Online Newsletter</A>
<LI><A HREF="http://www.will-harris.com/whh.htm">Will-Harris
House</A>
<LI><A
HREF="http://www.yahoo.com/Computers_and_Internet/Desktop_Publish
ing">Yahoo's listing of Desktop Publishing Resources</A>.
</UL>
</Body>
<IMG HEIGHT=200 WIDTH=145 Align=Right SRC="pen_ink.gif">
<HR><P>
<IMG HEIGHT=50 WIDTH=48 SRC="h.gif"><Strong>Back to Home
Page</Strong><P>

<Address>http://www.casey.mudville.net/fig128.htm<BR>
Last updated January 1, 1996 by John Maxymuk<P>
Please e-mail any comments or suggestions to:<BR>
<A
HREF="mailto:maxymuk@crab.rutgers.edu">maxymuk@crab.rutgers.edu
</A></Address>
</HTML>
```

13 DESKTOP PUBLISHING IS FOR YOUR LIBRARY

Computers have changed our lives dramatically, greatly increasing our creative outlets and productive capabilities. One clear example of this is desktop publishing. Fifteen years ago, if you wanted to create a newsletter or library guide, you'd have to type up the text on a typewriter (electric, only if you were lucky), round up any graphics you planned on using and hack out a cut-and-paste layout over a light table. Or you could pass on the layout duties to a service bureau or print shop. Ten years ago, you could at least enter your text into a primitive word processing program, but the layout options were still largely manual. Mac users could experiment with the fledgling page-layout program, PageMaker. Five years ago, the World Wide Web was just barely being spun.

Technological advances have been swift. Word processing software now not only processes words but also can handle graphics and provide rudimentary page layout. Page-layout software is so advanced that whole books (including this one) are designed using it; it is so easy to use that newsletters and other paper publications proliferate as never before. If you have page-layout software and a laser printer, then Gutenberg has come to your desktop. The World Wide Web, meanwhile, threatens to alter our vision of the world, as businesses, governmental agencies, and educational institutions race to establish meaningful presences on the Web.

DESKTOP PUBLISHING POSSIBILITIES

What we have covered in this book is how to harness these advances of the recent past to better disseminate relevant information in a variety of forms. Newsletters comprise a very flexible form that requires page-layout software to fully take advantage of its facilities. Newsletters from the desktop can pinpoint a certain message to a specific audience in an inviting and inventive way. They can incorporate photographs, illustrations, charts, tables, borders, boxes, and color seamlessly and appealingly.

Library guides generally utilize a more functional design. They can be produced skillfully on either good word processing or page-layout software. While graphic elements should be integrated into the page design whenever possible, they will usually take the form of small accents or enhancements. They must not detract from the text. Typographic consistency and style are essential.

Pages on the WWW can be produced using the most basic of text editors, but they can still include the widest variety of multimedia features—images, sound, and animation. What you must master is writing HTML programming code to mark up your text so that your digital pages will display handsomely on the screen and function well as links to other pages anywhere on the Web from anywhere in the world. The publication process is primarily an exercise in the effective organization of information.

There are so many other publishing possibilities for libraries that we have not covered. Flyers, posters, and agendas for upcoming meetings or events can be engagingly designed on your desktop. Maps and signs can be created with accuracy and clarity. Brochures and pamphlets can be produced to take advantage of paper sizes and folding styles. Forms can be developed for all sorts of library uses such as interlibrary loan and book request suggestions. Reports, proposals, stationery, correspondence, and surveys can all be devised easily to meet your library's needs. Any sort of publication you can conceive of you can publish on your desktop.

DESKTOP PUBLISHING PRINCIPLES

What all of these publications have in common is a series of principles. The text should make sense, and the type should be readable and legible. Typefaces should be few, fit well together, and reflect the right tone for the publication. White space should be ample enough so that the page does not look cluttered and is easy to read. Graphics should be large enough to view clearly, but not so large or plentiful that they overwhelm the page. Graphics should be chosen carefully for their quality as well as their suitability to the textual content. The mix of text, white space, and graphics should be balanced, consistent, and pleasing. Overall, the page should attract the reader, direct the reader's eyes to points of emphasis, and hold his or her attention. Above all, keep it simple; the style should serve the substance.

The most important common principle is conveying a meaningful message to a target audience. The elaborate layouts that desktop publishing allows you to create for a newsletter or library guide and the animated bells and whistles that HTML lets you merge into your Web page are wonderful, but they should underscore your message. They should not merely stress how clever the designer is.

THE MEDIUM IS NOT THE MESSAGE

Your primary emphasis in any publishing project, desktop or otherwise, must be good writing. The overall design is of paramount importance, but graphics and multimedia play subordinate roles to the text. The words must make sense and be written with enough vitality to be of interest. Grammar, punctuation, and spelling should be flawless so as not to detract from the message. A clear writing style should be evident.

The writer needs to know who the audience is, what they want to know, and what they need to know. The writer needs to be aware of the appropriate tone for this audience and this message. The information should be organized so as to be most easily understood by readers. The writer should streamline the text and not overwhelm readers by including every piece of information in any particular publication. In short, the text should be accurate, concise, and worthy of attention.

What desktop publishing allows you to do with good writing is accent it. Well-written words typed on a sheet of paper are of no value if they are not read by the intended audience. An attractively laid out and designed publication is more likely to be read. If it is intelligently distributed to a target audience, the chances of the message being received increase substantially. Libraries of all types are in the business of disseminating valuable information in many forms to their users. Because of the advances in desktop publishing, we are able to create new forums of useful information for our users.

What will guide us to create new forums of useful information? As Rod Serling would say on *The Twilight Zone,* "There is a fifth dimension beyond that which is known to man. It is a dimension as vast as space and as timeless as infinity. . . . This is the dimension of imagination." Desktop publishing offers you the opportunity to use your imagination, be productive, and have fun in the library.

A SELECT BIBLIOGRAPHY

SECTION 1: DESKTOP PUBLISHING BASICS

Barker, Malcolm E. *Book Design and Production for the Small Publisher.* San Francisco: Londonborn Publications, 1990.

Baudin, Fernand. *How Typography Works: And Why It Is Important.* New York: Design Press, 1989.

Browne, David. *Welcome to . . . Desktop Publishing.* New York: MIS Press, 1993.

Hewson, David. *Introduction to Desktop Publishing: A Guide to Buying and Using a Desktop Publishing System.* San Francisco: Chronicle Books, 1988.

Kleper, Michael L. *The Illustrated Handbook of Desktop Publishing and Typesetting.* Blue Ridge, PA: Windcrest, 1990.

Laing, John, ed. *Do-It-Yourself Graphic Design.* New York: Facts on File, 1984.

Miles, John. *Design for Desktop Publishing: A Guide to Layout and Typography on the Personal Computer.* San Francisco: Chronicle Books, 1987.

Moen, Daryl R. *Newspaper Layout and Design.* Ames, IA: Iowa State University Press, 1989.

Quilliam, Susan, and Ian Grove-Stephensen. *Into Print.* London: BBC Books, 1990.

Searfoss, Glenn. *The Computer Font Book.* Berkeley, CA: Osborne McGraw-Hill, 1993.

A FEW HELPFUL WWW SITES OF NOTE . . .

DTP by Lee
http://www.av.net/~bennett/

DTP Internet Jump List
http://www.teleport.com/~eidos/dtpij/dtpij.html

GetInfo DTP Online Newsletter
http://www.winternet.com/~jmg/Getinfo.html

Will-Harris House
http://getinfo.asap.net/

Yahoo Desktop Publishing Resources
http://www.yahoo.com/Computers_and_Internet/
Desktop_Publishing

SECTION 2: NEWSLETTERS

Bivins, Thomas, and William Ryan. *How to Produce Creative Publications: Traditional Techniques and Computer Applications.* Lincolnwood, IL: NTC Business Books, 1990.

Blake, Barbara Radke, and Barbara L. Stein. *Creating Newsletters, Brochures, and Pamphlets: A How-To-Do-It Manual.* New York: Neal-Schuman, 1992.

Parker, Roger C. *Looking Good in Print: A Guide to Basic Design for Desktop Publishing.* Chapel Hill, NC: Ventana Press, 1990.

————. *The Makeover Book: 101 Design Solutions for Desktop Publishing.* Chapel Hill, NC: Ventana Press, 1989.

————. *Newsletters from the Desktop: Designing Effective Publications with your Computer.* Chapel Hill, NC: Ventana Press, 1990.

Shusan, Ronnie, and Don Wright. *Desktop Publishing by Design.* Redmond, WA: Microsoft Press, 1991.

SECTION 3: LIBRARY GUIDES

Branch, Katherine, ed. *Sourcebook for Bibliographic Instruction.* Chicago: Bibliographic Instruction Section, Association of College and Research Libraries, 1993.

Cubberley, Carol W. "Write Procedures that Work." *Library Journal*, September 15, 1991, v116: 42–45.

Edsall, Marian S. *Library Promotion Handbook.* Phoenix, AZ: Oryx Press, 1980.

Hartley, James. *Designing Instructional Text.* London: Kogan Page, 1978.

Jackson, William J. "The User-Friendly Library Guide." *C & RL News*, October 1984, v45 (9): 468–71.

MacDonald, Linda Brew . . . et al. *Teaching Technologies in Libraries: A Practical Guide.* Boston: G. K. Hall, 1991.

Peterson, Lorna, and Jamie W. Coniglio. "Readability of Selected Academic Library Guides." *RQ*, Winter 1987: 233–39.

Pratt, Henry J. "Tips on Writing the How-To Article." *Writer*, September 1989, v102 (9): 31–32.

Renford, Beverly, and Linnea Hendrickson. *Bibliographic Instruction: A Handbook.* New York: Neal-Schuman, 1980.

Roberts, Anne F., and Susan G. Blandy. *Library Instruction for Librarians*. Englewood, CO: Libraries Unlimited, Inc., 1989.

Slatkin, Elizabeth. *How to Write a Manual*. Berkeley, CA: Ten Speed Press, 1991.

Weiss, Edmond H. *How to Write a Usable User Manual*. Philadelphia, PA: ISI Press, 1985.

Williams, Joseph M. *Style: Toward Clarity and Grace*. Chicago: University of Chicago Press, 1990.

SECTION 4: WORLD WIDE WEB PAGES

Aronson, Larry. *HTML Manual of Style*. Emeryville, CA: Ziff-Davis, 1994.

December, John, and Neil Randall. *The World Wide Web Unleashed*. Indianapolis, IN: Sams Publishing, 1995.

Hockey, Susan. "From the Editor: Text Is More Than Just Words on the Page." *D-Lib*, November 1995. (*D-Lib* is published only on the WWW at http://www.dlib.org/dlib/)

Horton, William, et al. *The Web Page Design Cookbook: All the Ingredients You Need to Create 5-Star Web Pages*. New York: Wiley, 1996.

LeJeune, Urban. *Netscape & HTML Explorer*. Scottsdale, AZ: Coriolis Group, 1995.

LeMay, Laura. *Teach Yourself Web Publishing with HTML in a Week*. Indianapolis, IN: Sams Publishing, 1995.

———. *Teach Yourself More Web Publishing with HTML in a Week*. Indianapolis, IN: Sams Publishing, 1995.

McLeod, Jennifer, and Michael White. "Building the Virtual Campus Bit By Bit: World Wide Web Development at the University of Maine." *Computers in Libraries*, November/December 1995, v15 (10): 45–49.

Metz, Ray E., and Gail Junion-Metz. *Using the World Wide Web and Creating Home Pages: A How-To-Do-It Manual for Librarians*. New York: Neal-Schuman, 1996.

Taylor, Dave. *Creating Cool Web Pages with HTML*. Foster City, CA: IDG Books, 1995.

A FEW HELPFUL WWW SITES . . .

A Beginner's Guide to HTML
http://www.ncsa.uiuc.edu/General/Internet/WWW/
HTMLPrimer.html

Composing Good HTML
http://www.cs.cmu.edu/~tilt/cgh/

Don Siegel's Tips
http://www.dsiegel/com/tips

How Do They Do That with HTML?
http://www.nashville.net/~carl/htmlguide/index.html

How to Publish on the World Wide Web
http://www.thegiim.org/

HTML Bad Style Page
http://www.earth.com/bad-style/

The HTML Writers Guild: Principles of Good HTML Design
http://ugweb.cs.ualberta.ca/~gerald/guild/style.html

The Only HTML Information Page You Really Need
http://www.ocala.com/~bombadil/nuthin/yahoo.htm

Putting Information on the Web
http://www.w3.org/hypertext/WWW/Provider/Overview.html

Teaching a New Dog Old Tricks: A Macintosh-Based World Wide Web Starter Kit Featuring MacHTTP and Other Tools
http://152.1.24.177/teaching/manuscript

Urb's Home Page
http://www.charm.net/~lejeune/

Web Style Manual from the Yale Center for Advanced Instructional Media
http://info.med.yale.edu/caim/StyleManual_Top.HTML

Yahoo World Wide Web Resources
http://www.yahoo.com/Computers_and_Internet/Internet/World_Wide_Web

INDEX

COLOPHON

John Maxymuk is a reference librarian responsible for micro-computers, government documents, and circulation at the Paul Robeson Library on the Camden Campus of Rutgers University. He has 10 years of desktop publishing experience, 15 years of library experience, and 20 years of writing and editing experience. In addition to newsletters, handouts, and web pages, he has published articles, reviews, and other pieces. This is his third book. His homepage is at http://www.rci.rutgers.edu/~maxymuk/home/home.html.